THE GUIDE TO THE FA
CARLING PREMIERSHIP

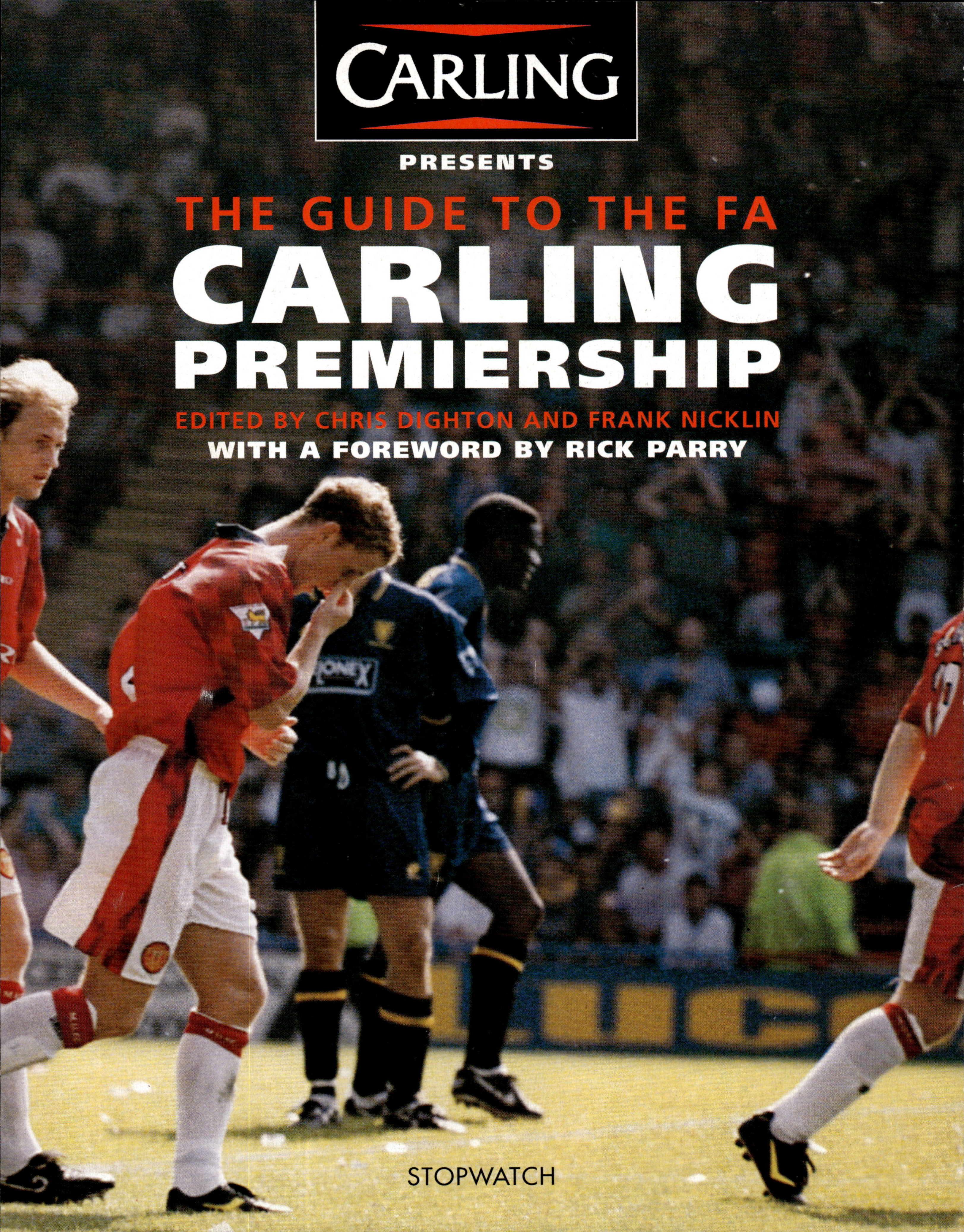

CARLING
PRESENTS
THE GUIDE TO THE FA
CARLING
PREMIERSHIP
EDITED BY CHRIS DIGHTON AND FRANK NICKLIN
WITH A FOREWORD BY RICK PARRY
STOPWATCH

List of Contents

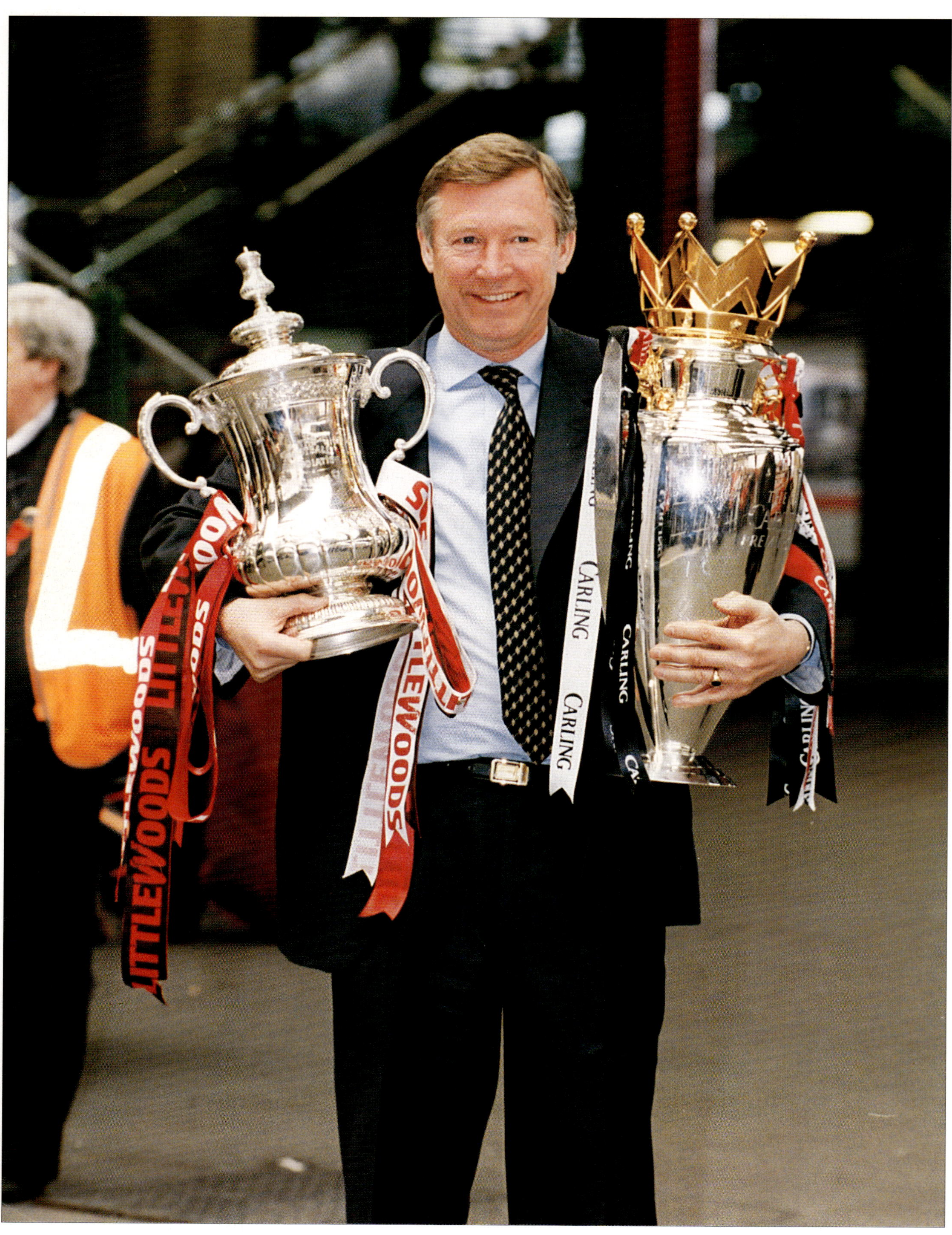

The pace of change has been incredible

says Rick Parry, Chief Executive of the Premier League

Football is a modern revolution, a sweeping movement of the 1990s eager to embrace changing technologies, advance into new markets and stand at the cutting edge of the rapidly changing face of television.

Since the Premier League started in the 1992–93 season, football has changed beyond recognition on all fronts: from the players in the game, to how we watch it, where we watch and the facilities provided for spectating. Above all that, the game today is in the grip of Klondyke fever. And according to Rick Parry, Chief Executive of the Premier League, we ain't seen nothing yet.

So much from a game that has been around for so long and is beautiful for its simplicity – but then so was the wheel and look how that changed our lives.

Rick Parry

Yet for all the advances made and all the advances to come, Parry insists that there is nothing to beat being there, the adrenalin of the occasion is unique.

"When the fixture list came out in July I was quickly going through it to see who was playing where. The prospect of Middlesbrough against Chelsea, Fabrizio Ravanelli up against Gianluca Vialli, has to be a mouth-watering treat for football fans.

"That is just one game of dozens that spark the imagination and for all that television does for the sport, football is a game about being at the ground to see it live, to take in that atmosphere which just cannot be transmitted into the home by a television camera. Television stimulates interest but is not more attractive than being present.

Just good friends. Gianluca Vialli (*above*) and Fabrizio Ravanelli (*left*), close team-mates at Juventus but now rivals in the Premiership.

"The pace of change has been incredible, crowds have risen season–on–season since the Premier League started and some of the biggest names in world football are wanting to play in England.

"Yet in many ways this is the beginning, there is room for more growth and new technology will change again how we see the game. It would take more than a brave man to predict exactly what will happen because the scope is so enormous.

"There is digital TV which not only produces more channels but also greatly enhances the quality of the picture. That might not do much for a political debate but for sport, and for football, it provides another opportunity.

"And you have to wonder where in the information highway will the Internet and the rest lead us. It is quite conceivable that in a few years you could watch Southampton play, see Matthew Le Tissier score a goal and call back on

Opposite: Manchester United manager Alex Ferguson on show with the trophies signalling the supreme double of the Premiership title and FA Cup.

Karel Poborsky

Roberto Di Matteo

replay the last ten goals he has scored. From where we stand now the possibilities seem infinite."

For all that has happened and all that will happen, Parry remains pragmatic and standing steady while the game is flooded by money, TV deals that have put £9 million into the pockets of the Premiership clubs and reported wage deals that appear gilded by Hollywood legend.

The cynics say that boom leads to crash but Parry, while accepting everything is finite, says that football is still on an upward curve, developing and learning all the time.

"It is hard work keeping pace but that is a good problem to have, I'd much rather be in this position than a stagnant one. Our job is to make sure that the game develops in the right way and I have to say that in every aspect clubs today are far more professional than they were when the Premier League began.

"We have a responsibility to take care of the development of the game for youngsters, create coaching, marketing and promotion infrastructures. We also listen to the supporters because they, after all, are the customers and they are by nature very conservative.

"We are not going to stand still and the statistics show that the Premiership is providing people with what they want. There was controversy over the introduction of all-seater stadia but gates rose and one of the first things I do after a Premiership Saturday is check the attendances.

"And this climb has happened against a background of rising ticket prices beyond the rate of inflation.

"When the Premier League first started, people said that it was just the First Division with a new name but it was always going to take three or four years to establish itself. Now those same people say the gulf between the Premiership and the First Division is too big. But you can't have it both ways.

"Of course we are aware of the widening gulf and we are watching the position but really the top sides set an example for the others to aspire to. Even within the Premiership there is room for the big, medium and small-sized clubs and the fact is that at the moment it is working.

"Some of the less affluent clubs in the Premiership are worried about the transfer fees and wages being paid by the larger clubs but then along comes another TV deal and everyone is richer and happier for a while.

"The real test of what is going on is on the field and there is no doubt that the football in this country is exciting.

"Two seasons ago we had the drama of Blackburn winning the title and then, in the 1995-96 season, we reached the final day of Premiership matches where every game – bar one – had an effect on the championship, European places and relegation issues. That's breathtaking stuff.

"Manchester United have won three out of the four Premiership titles but never really run away with it in the way Liverpool were the top side in the 1980s. In the Premiership, there have been worthy challengers along the way in every season and I would say in England the top division is more competitive than abroad.

"In Italy there are five top sides, Spain have three or four while the Dutch, Belgians and to a lesser extent the French have even fewer who are genuine winners."

Europe, the Bosman decision and the influx of top players, like Ravanelli, Vialli, Franck Leboeuf, Roberto Di Matteo, Karel Poborksy to join Eric Cantona, Ruud Gullit, Dennis Bergkamp, Faustino Asprilla and Juninho already here, have all added to the changing face of the English game but not to the detriment of it, says Parry.

He argues that while the foreign players bring an exotic touch the good English players will still succeed.

"There is no doubt that there is a bigger risk with a foreign player because of the culture differences, the language barriers – they have far more to contend with and consequently are a greater risk," he says.

"That is why we need to concern ourselves with the development of the game from the very bottom.

"As far as the Bosman case goes, that ruling clarified what already existed in European law regarding the freedom of workers within the European Community. We can only rise to the challenge it presents by producing our own better young players."

In a world of such rapid change the grand traditions that are part of the game could well be lost but without being sentimental about it, Parry says the past needs, at times, the safety of a preservation order.

"There is no need for change for changes sake but on the other side of the coin you cannot blindly carry on as you have been. Just because it worked in the 1870s or 1970s does not mean it is going to work today and if something can be improved, then do it.

"But as I say, the supporters are conservative and their needs always have to be taken into consideration. The fact that more women and children are going to matches is encouraging and there is a growing foreign audience."

The success of Euro'96 has added icing to the cake but Parry remains sanguine about the effect it has had on the Premiership in terms of England's success.

"If England had done badly it would not have had a cataclysmic effect on the Premiership; our success did not depend on the success of the national team because we were strong in the first place," he says.

"That England did well was marvellous but I think that the live audience for the tournament was very different to the one that attends Premiership games week-in and week-out during the season."

And so the beautiful game rides on, cresting a boom that seems to have no end. Parry, however, agrees that the business of football, as it is for the teams on the pitch, is a risk business and it is the fear of failure which will help to keep it on the straight and narrow.

Parry, by profession an accountant, approaches the constantly shifting conundrums of his job with a cool detachment which belies his obvious passion for football and heartfelt concern for its welfare.

"Professionalism in marketing football is a new phenomenon and we don't know where the peak is, but clubs have got to act in a responsible way. It is a business and the consequences for getting it wrong are obvious," he adds.

"The Premiership has worked because everyone has pulled together, the clubs have an equal voice and there are no hidden agendas."

Parry played for Cheshire schoolboys in his youth and went on to have a trial with Liverpool, but he did not progress at Anfield so he then made a series of appearances for the Everton juniors. That too fizzled out and he went on to qualify as a chartered accountant in 1979. Along the way to Lancaster Gate, headquarters of the Premiership, he has worked in tourism in Suffolk, been involved in two Olympic bids by Manchester then gone on to work for the Football League in Lytham St Annes.

His passion for the game remains as strong today as it did in his youth and he says that if he had his time again he would give professional football another shot, before adding: "Who wouldn't? It is the sport everyone wants to play."

Parry, it should be noted, was a goalkeeper and it seems that any which way his career went, the end result would have been the same – he was always destined to have his hands full.

Euro '96 brought together many Premiership stars. Here Gary McAllister, the Scotland skipper, is flying high over his England rival Paul Ince.

The party's over as Germany celebrate their entry to the Euro '96 final after that unforgettable, almost unbearable, penalty shoot-out.

Rick Parry was interviewed by Chris Dighton.

The Legacy of Euro '96

by Aubrey Ganguly

So football finally came home. England may not have won the 1996 European Championship, but surely not since 1966 has the nation felt such an overwhelming sense of pride and joy in the national game.

Three weeks of good weather, high spirits and great football, plus some of the finest performances seen from an England team in 30 years, combined to re-affirm the "beautiful game" as the world's finest sport.

When the heartbreak of the penalty shoot-out against Germany subsided, the country was left with a new-found confidence that once again England can compete on the world stage.

But as that grand occasion fades to a pleasant memory and the World Cup campaign for 1998 in France comes to the fore, Euro'96 will leave behind more than just a transient optimism. Having hosted such a major tournament, certain questions should be asked about its impact on English football. How will it affect the domestic game? Does it mean Premiership clubs can once again be a force in European competition? And, most pertinently, how will it influence the England team as they attempt to qualify for France?

Of the three, the first question is probably the easiest to answer. Following any European Championship or World Cup, transfer speculation is always rife. Like all good tournaments, Euro'96 provided more than its fair share of stars and canny Premiership managers watched with cheque books open, keen to bring a few new faces to their particular club.

There were certainly plenty of contenders. Wonder goals from the Czech Republic's Karel Poborsky and Croatia's Davor Suker put both players in the spotlight, while the solid defending of Spain's Sergi Barjuan also won many admirers.

Marcel Desailly was one of the few French players to live up to expectations, with some fine performances in the tournament, and Portugal's Joao Pinto was excellent throughout.

England too, had their share of stars. David Seaman firmly established himself as the No 1 goalkeeper at Euro'96, while Steve McManaman was a revelation attacking from the wings. And Alan Shearer reminded everyone just why he's without doubt the Premiership's finest striker with five goals that earned him the Golden Boot.

Of course, the Press had a field day. Anyone who kicked a ball was suddenly "being targeted" by one club or another. But when the dust settled, a number of interesting foreign signings had been made, the biggest of which was undoubtedly the £7 million transfer of Fabrizio Ravanelli from Juventus to Middlesbrough. The signing of the Italian was a real coup for 'Boro manager Bryan Robson. Along with the arrival of compatriots Gianluca Vialli and

Pure joy for Alan Shearer and millions of home fans as he gives England the lead, sadly short-lived, against a torn-apart German defence.

A tense meeting between rivals at club and country level. John Collins (Celtic and Scotland) rides the challenge of Paul Gascoigne (Rangers and England).

On the ball as ever. Alan Shearer plunges in with a brilliant header to put England in front against the Auld Enemy.

Roberto Di Matteo, both to Chelsea, it sparked cries of an Italian invasion and was said by some to be proof that the Premiership is now Europe's biggest draw, the best league in the world, better even than the Italian Serie A.

However, cynics point out that Vialli is now the wrong side of 30 and, like Paulo Futre, West Ham's signing from AC Milan, he may face accusations of coming to England for one final big pay day before ending his career.

Whatever the reasoning behind the moves though, players of such calibre don't become bad overnight and will surely have much to offer the Premiership. Ruud Gullit, no spring chicken himself and in his mid-30s, is living proof of that. With his best years behind him, he was still many people's choice for player of the year in the 1995-96 season and provides a good indication of how foreign players can contribute to the development of a Premier club.

Ravanelli, Di Matteo, Poborksy, Jerkan, Raducioiu, Leboeuf and Asanovic were all plucked from Euro '96 for the Premiership. Together with other new foreign signings Emerson, Vialli, Donis and Futre among them, they add a cosmopolitan edge to English football that should help in the push to make English clubs again a force in the European arena.

With the UEFA limitation on the number of "foreign" players now scrapped, clubs will be able to field their preferred side in European competitions for the first time, without any of the complicated team juggling that has previously blighted the likes of Manchester United, among others, in sustaining a concerted campaign.

The influx of foreign players to these shores, as well as being an attractive proposition to fans, should also prove advantageous to British players. Competing against the crop of European talent on a week-in, week-out basis can only be beneficial to home-grown talent, both in their individual play and their tactical awareness.

One of the many delights of Euro '96 was the plethora of different playing styles and tactics employed. Between the attractive passing of the Portuguese, the flexibility of the Germans, the solid organisation of the French and the sweeping attacks of the Croats, practically every style of play was on view. England, too, showed a tactical awareness and willingness to adapt that few suspected they were capable of before the tournament began.

Terry Venables was keen to pick players who could perform more than one task, and play in more than one position. He described his England line-up as a team for all seasons. "If it is a battle, we can handle that. If it is a football match, we can be intelligent and pull opponents out of position and make chances."

If English clubs are to improve on their recent, rather poor, showing in Europe, they too will have to show a willingness to adapt their game as needs dictate.

As Blackburn manager Ray Harford said in the late autumn of 1995, after his club's underwhelming performance in Europe: "We've played three teams in the past week and they all played with two markers and a sweeper, but they each played it differently. And what really impressed me was the amount of ground every player covers, both with the ball and without it.

"It's not just that they counter-attack, but they do it with such pace that you feel swamped. They break out with such freedom of movement."

If the Premiership wants to lay any real claim to being the best league in the world, it will have to improve its success rate in Europe. Currently it still lags some way behind Italy's Serie A. In the five seasons from 1991 to 1995, English clubs reached three European finals – through Arsenal (twice) and Manchester United. In the same period, Italian clubs reached 13 finals.

Euro '96, however, has provided the perfect platform from which to launch a new challenge. Practically all Premiership clubs have now discarded the old four-man defence for a more flexible three-man system, with additional players on either flank.

As Terry Venables' side showed at Wembley, this allows the team to switch from defence to attack in seconds. Of course, in order for it to work, players must know their role in the team.

On their way to winning Euro '96, Germany provided an excellent example of this flexibility at work. Time and time again, the German attack was bolstered by their superb sweeper Matthias Sammer, who seemed to drift upfield at will to create all sorts of problems for the opposition. Crucially, though, if a German attack broke down, there never seemed to be any holes in their defence to exploit.

If the European Championship does prove to have an impact on the Premiership then, tactically, this is where it will be. Manchester United, Newcastle and Liverpool have all been playing with defenders that bolster the attack for some time, and Chelsea have been developing their own brand of "Continental-style" football over the last season or two, but it's probably only now that we'll begin to see the majority of clubs adopt a more flexible formation.

Of course the legacy of Euro '96 is more than the mere tangibles of tactics and transfers. The event and, more specifically, England's performance has restored a self-belief within the squad and a level of support from the nation not seen for many years.

It's not hard to see why. Before 1996, England's record in the European Championship competition was pretty dreadful. In 1992 they managed only a draw and two defeats, 1988 saw three defeats and in 1984 they failed even to qualify for the tournament. The 1994 World Cup, too, carried on without England.

This time things were different. An impressive first half against Switzerland set the tone. After a dozen internationals without a goal, Alan Shearer ended his barren spell when it counted, with a blistering shot to put England ahead. Although England faltered in the latter stages of the match to concede a draw, they bounced back immediately against the "auld enemy" to gain a valuable 2-0 win over Scotland.

Paul Gascoigne made his critics eat their words with one of the best goals in Wembley's history and Shearer was once again on the score sheet. England were on their way but the best was yet to come.

It's England 4, Holland 1. Fantastic!

Swiss miss tackle on Shearer.

Gascoigne – subdued as ever.

A penalty saved . . .

A penalty scored . . .

. . . but, sadly, a penalty missed.

The match against Holland was next and will perhaps be the one that remains longest in the memory. If a nation's fortunes really can be turned around in 90 minutes, then this was the occasion. The Dutch had rightly been acclaimed as one of the best sides in Europe and played the kind of football that England, and English clubs, aspire to, full of good passing and movement from tactically-aware players.

Terry Venables' men came into the match hoping for at least a draw but finished it convincing winners with a breathtaking performance that had even those hardened hacks of the football press singing their praises. After taking the lead through an Alan Shearer penalty, a rampant England tore Holland apart with a display of passing, movement, ball-skills and finishing that meant more to English football than any result since 1966. Two goals from Sheringham and another from Shearer ensured a 4–1 win that in one fell swoop started a surge of passion in the national game.

"England taught us a lesson in every aspect of the game, in offence and defence," said a shell-shocked Guus Hiddink, the Dutch coach, after the match. But more importantly, it offered both club and country a glimpse of what can be achieved if English football continues to develop.

A tight quarter-final against Spain followed, but England held their nerve during the penalty shoot-out to reach a semi-final encounter with Germany. And although penalties eventually put them out of the tournament in that match, it was not before yet another stirring perfomance from England, who clearly believed they could win the competition.

An early goal from Shearer had English hopes rising but the Germans remained focused and eventually got the equaliser that took the game into extra time. An agonising 30 minutes followed as both sides went all out for the "golden goal" that would take them to the final. But although England twice came close, it was the Germans who ran out winners after the spot-kicks.

England, however, had made their point. They were once again a team to fear. Even the Germans acknowledged as much, with Franz Beckenbauer saying: "England have the potential to win the next World Cup. That's how highly I now rate them."

Countryman Jurgen Klinsmann was also quick to point out England's prospects. "Terry Venables has left Glenn Hoddle a team which suddenly has become one of the strongest in the world," said the former Tottenham striker. "You only have to look at the way England played different opposition to realise the good job he did. English football has respect now, and other countries will not look forward to playing them."

Venables, perhaps not wishing to put pressure on his successor, was more restrained after the tournament, but he agreed that England's prospects look good. "There is a good nucleus of players now, there is no doubt about that," he said. "They have that good feeling, knowing they can play anyone on equal terms. There was a time when we wondered how many teams like Germany, Spain and Holland might beat us. Now we expect to beat them."

If Venables is correct, then there's a lot to look forward to in the next few years, and perhaps that's the true legacy of Euro '96.

On the domestic front, the Premiership, already acknowledged as the most exciting in the world, now looks set to improve further. The influx of quality foreign players and a growing sophistication can only increase the quality of football. That in turn spells good news for clubs battling to gain European honours. And on the international scene, England now seem to have their healthiest prospects for some decades.

In the words of the song: "Thirty years of hurt, never stopped me dreaming. . ."

The Premiership Teams – Facts and Figures

Tony Adams

1992-93

PRE-SEASON: Arsenal sell David Rocastle to Leeds for £2 million and a young Andy Cole to Bristol City for only £500,000. Cole would later go to Newcastle for £1.75 million.

THE SEASON: Arsenal's first Premier League game is at Norwich, where they relinquish a 2-0 lead to end the game with a 4-2 defeat. They record their first victory at Anfield, where Wright scores his first of 15 League goals.

In November, Arsenal top the table after six consecutive victories, but slip to ninth by the end of the year after a goal drought.

In February, they strengthen their defence with the arrival of Martin Keown from Everton for £2 million. He replaces Steve Bould at the back.

Arsenal finish their first Premier League season in tenth position after a disappointing 1993. They have 56 points from 42 matches, having recorded 15 wins and 11 draws.

Best wins 3-0 against Coventry in November and Crystal Palace in May; worst defeat 3-0 at Leeds in November. Top scorer: Ian Wright (15).

Paul Merson

1993-94

PRE-SEASON: Arsenal pay £1 million to Crystal Palace for the midfielder, Eddie McGoldrick, who quickly gains a regular place in the side.

THE SEASON: Arsenal improve greatly on their previous season, finishing fourth. They were still, however, 19 points behind the winners, Manchester United.

They have a disappointing start to 1993-94, losing 3-0 at home to Coventry, but recover to win the North London derby against Spurs with a goal from Ian Wright. He goes on to score 23 goals in the League.

The Highbury club remains unbeaten in 1994 for the rest of the season, guaranteeing a speedy rise up the Premiership. They finish the season with 17 draws, conceding only 13 goals away from home, which is testimony to their solid defence.

Best wins 5-1 and 4-0 in their two games against Ipswich; worst defeat the opening 3-0 thrashing at the hands of Coventry. Top scorer: Ian Wright (23).

Arsenal facts and figures

CLUB ADDRESS: Arsenal Stadium, Highbury, London N5 1BU.

TELEPHONE: 0171-226 0304

FAX: 0171-226 0329

CLUBLINE: 0891-20 20 20

The club was formed in 1886, turning professional in 1893.

PREVIOUS GROUNDS: Plumstead Common, Sportsman Ground, Manor Ground and Invicta Ground.

The club was previously called Dial Square, Royal Arsenal and Woolwich Arsenal.

RECORD ATTENDANCE: 73,295 v Sunderland, Div 1, March 1935.

BIGGEST WIN: 12-0 v Loughborough Town, Div 2, March 1900.

BIGGEST DEFEAT: 0-8 v Loughborough Town, Div 2, December 1896.

TOP LEAGUE SCORER IN SEASON: Ted Drake (42), 1934-35.

HIGHEST AGGREGATE SCORER: Cliff Bastin (150), 1930-46.

MOST CAPPED PLAYER: Kenny Sansom (86) for England.

STARS OF YESTERYEAR: Alex James (1929-37), Cliff Bastin (1930-46), Ted Drake (1934-39), Joe Mercer (1946-54), Don Howe (1964-66), Liam Brady (1973-80), Frank Stapleton (1973-80).

GREAT MANAGERS: Herbert Chapman

1994-95

PRE-SEASON: There is little transfer movement at Highbury, the only arrival being Stefan Schwarz, a transfer that was to prove controversial.

THE SEASON: Activities on the field for Arsenal are overshadowed by events off the pitch. George Graham loses his manager's position in February after investigations by the FA into allegations of illegal transfer deals.

In November, Paul Merson reveals his drink, drugs and gambling problems and leaves the game for a few months to rehabilitate. Arsenal miss his skill in midfield.

Wright once again finishes the season as top scorer but Arsenal still languish in the middle of the table. New arrivals in the form of John Hartson, Chris Kiwomya and Glenn Helder cannot rescue the season.

They finish 1994-95 with 51 points, having won only 13 games.

Best win 5-1 at home to Norwich in April; worst defeat by a three-goal deficit at Anfield. Top scorer: Ian Wright (18).

1995-96

PRE-SEASON: Bruce Rioch is appointed manager and Arsenal are not to be left behind as English clubs turn to Europe for star signings. Dennis Bergkamp joins for £7.5 million from Inter Milan and David Platt comes from Sampdoria for £4.75 million.

THE SEASON: European football for the 1996-97 season is guaranteed late on in the last match of the season as Dennis Bergkamp scores the winning goal in a 2-1 victory over already-relegated Bolton. It is enough to give Arsenal fifth place in the Premiership and a place in the Uefa Cup.

The club made a solid start to the season, unbeaten in their first seven games but then losing 1-0 at Chelsea.

Home victories over eventual champions Manchester United and second-placed Newcastle showed what might have been but for some surprising defeats, away at Bolton and Sheffield Wednesday and at home to Everton.

Best wins 3-0 away at Leeds and Wimbledon and home to QPR; worst defeat 1-3 at Liverpool and home to Wimbledon. Top scorer: Ian Wright (15).

Five days before the start of the new 1996-97 season Arsenal sacked manager Bruce Rioch. He was replaced by Frenchman Arsene Wenger, coach to Grampus Eight, Gary Lineker's old club in Japan, and former coach of French champions Monaco.

THE MANAGERS: George Graham 1986-95, Bruce Rioch 1995-96, Arsène Wenger 1996-

(1925-34), Tom Whittaker (1947-1956), Bertie Mee (1966-76), George Graham (1986-95).

HONOURS: 1929-30 – FA Cup winners,
1930-31 – First Division champions,
1932-33 – First Division champions,
1933-34 – First Division champions,
1934-35 – First Division champions,
1935-36 – FA Cup winners,
1937-38 – First Division champions,
1947-48 – First Division champions,
1949-50 – FA Cup winners,
1952-53 – First Division champions,
1969-70 – Fairs Cup winners,
1970-71 – First Division champions, FA Cup winners,
1978-79 – FA Cup winners,
1986-87 – League Cup winners,
1988-89 – First Division champions,
1990-91 – First Division champions,
1992-93 – FA Cup winners, League Cup winners,
1993-94 – European Cup-Winners' Cup winners.

Dwight Yorke

Left: Mark Draper
Right: Andy Townsend

ASTON VILLA
– The Premiership History

1992-93 PRE-SEASON: The purchase of experienced Ireland international Ray Houghton from Liverpool for £900,000 strengthens a Villa squad with a sound defence and a quality striker in Dalian Atkinson.

THE SEASON: Aston Villa draw their first three Premier League games 1-1 with all three goals coming from the boot of Atkinson. By February, they have climbed to second after losing only five games in the first 27 matches of the season.

It is now a two-horse race, with Aston Villa and Manchester United vying for the first Premier title. They buy Dean Saunders, who ends the season as leading scorer, and goalkeeper Mark Bosnich, who takes over from Nigel Spink.

After a spell at the top of the table, they finish runners-up after three defeats against Blackburn, Oldham and QPR. Manchester United win the League. Villa finish the season with 74 points, having won half of their 42 games but losing ten, a figure which proves decisive.

Best win 5-1 v Middlesbrough in September; worst defeat the 3-0 pounding at Blackburn which finalises their loss of the title. Top scorer: Dean Saunders (13).

1993-94 PRE-SEASON: After a successful first Premier season in which Saunders and Atkinson formed a deadly partnership, Ron Atkinson strengthens his squad with the purchase of Guy Whittingham from Portsmouth for £1.2 million, and also buys another Irish international in the person of Andy Townsend of Chelsea.

Aston Villa facts and figures

CLUB ADDRESS: Villa Park, Trinity Road, Birmingham B6 6HE.

TELEPHONE: 0121-327 5353

FAX: 0121-322 2107

NEWSLINE: 0891 202020

The club was formed in 1874, turning professional in 1896.

PREVIOUS GROUNDS: Aston Park and Perry Barr.

RECORD ATTENDANCE: 76,588 v Derby County, FA Cup 6th rnd, March 1946.

BIGGEST WIN: 13-0 v Wednesbury Old Ath in FA Cup 1st rnd, October 1886.

BIGGEST DEFEAT: 1-8 v Blackburn in FA Cup 3rd rnd, February 1889.

TOP LEAGUE SCORER IN A SEASON: 'Pongo' Waring (49), 1930-31.

HIGHEST AGGREGATE SCORER: Harry Hampton (215), 1904-20.

MOST CAPPED PLAYER: Paul McGrath (80) for Republic of Ireland.

STARS OF YESTERYEAR: Harry Hampton (1904-20), Frank Barson (1919-22), Billy Walker (1919-33), 'Pongo' Waring (1927-35), Peter McParland (1952-62), Andy Gray (1975-79 and 1985-87).

GREAT MANAGERS: Eric Houghton (1953-58), Ron Saunders (1974-82), Tony Barton (1982-84).

HONOURS: 1886-87 – FA Cup winners,
1893-94 – First Division champions,
1894-95 – FA Cup winners,
1895-96 – First Division champions,
1896-97 – First Division champions, FA Cup winners,
1898-99 – First Division champions,
1899-1900 – First Division champions,
1904-05 – FA Cup winners,
1909-10 – First Division champions,
1912-13 – FA Cup winners,
1919-20 – FA Cup winners,
1937-38 – Second Division champions,
1956-57 – FA Cup winners,
1959-60 – Second Division champions,
1960-61 – League Cup winners,
1971-72 – Third Division champions,
1974-75 – League Cup winners,
1976-77 – League Cup winners,
1980-81 – First Division champions,
1981-82 – European Cup winners,
1993-94 – League Cup winners,
1995-96 – League Cup winners.

 A disappointing League performance after the near-glory of the previous year, although Villa begin encouragingly with a 4-1 victory over QPR. Despite snatches of success, they fail to regain the momentum of 1992-93.

Saunders and Atkinson continue to score goals but the defence concedes 50 to leave Villa in tenth position at the end of the season, and with only the Coca-Cola Cup to give them hope of glory.

Their season ends on a total of 57 points, with them having lost 15 of their 42 games, eight of those at Villa Park.

Best win 5-0 v Swindon in October; worst defeat 3-1 at Old Trafford against the champions. Top scorer: Dean Saunders (10).

1994-95

PRE-SEASON: Ron Atkinson continues his quest for a striker to partner Saunders and Atkinson up front with the purchase of the Gladiators star, John Fashanu, for £1.35 million from Wimbledon.

THE SEASON: Villa, only two years after finishing second, fight a relegation battle and lose their manager of the last three years. A series of nine games without victory culminates in the dismissal of Ron Atkinson in November.

Brian Little, a former player, becomes the new manager after leading Leicester City into the division. Performances improve and Ian Taylor arrives from Sheffield Wednesday, to be joined by Tommy Johnson and Gary Charles from Derby County.

Villa then plummet from ninth to 18th after winning once in 11 games and scoring only three goals. Five points from their last three games, including a priceless victory over Liverpool, save them as they finish the season in 18th place, one above relegation, with 48 points. They had won only 11 of their 42 fixtures.

Best win 3-0 v Chelsea in December; worst defeat a 4-0 hammering at the hands of Leeds. Top scorer: Dean Saunders (15).

1995-96

PRE-SEASON: New faces aplenty at Aston Villa where Brian Little embarks on his first full season in charge. His three key signings are the Leicester midfielder Mark Draper for £3.25 million, and Crystal Palace midfielder-defender Gareth Southgate for £2.5 million. Savo Milosevic is bought for £3.5 million from Partizan Belgrade.

THE SEASON: The new-look Villa make a storming start – Manchester United are beaten 3-1 on the opening day, Tottenham are then defeated 1-0 at White Hart Lane.

A 2-0 slip at Leeds follows and while good wins at Coventry, Manchester City and West Ham are achieved, Villa ride high without really threatening the top three.

Home form is good, with just three defeats all season, but Villa's best moments come in the Coca-Cola Cup. They beat Arsenal on away goals in the semi-final following a 2-2 draw at Highbury and a 0-0 home leg then go on to beat Leeds decisively 3-0 at Wembley.

Inspired by Dwight Yorke's splendid goal-scoring feats, Villa can see through the season assured of European competition in 1996-97 and finish in the top ten. It is a vast improvement on the previous season when they were in danger of relegation right up to the last game of the season.

Best win 4-1 over Coventry at Villa Park in December; worst defeat 3-0 at Liverpool in March. Top scorer: Dwight Yorke (17).

THE MANAGERS: Ron Atkinson 1991-94, Brian Little 1994-

ASTON VILLA'S PREMIER SUPER TEN 1992-96

MARK BOSNICH: Australian international with a fine reputation in England. Born 13-1-72.

PAUL McGRATH: Solid defender and record Republic of Ireland international with 80 caps. Integral part of club and international teams. Born 4-12-59.

DEAN SAUNDERS: Welsh international whose goals helped Villa to their second place in 1992-93. Sold to Galatasaray for £2 million in 1995. Born 21-6-64.

DALIAN ATKINSON: Shrewsbury-born forward who began his career with Ipswich. After four years at Villa Park, he was sold to the Turkish side Fenerbahce for £1.25 million. Born 21-3-68.

DWIGHT YORKE: International with Trinidad and Tobago who had a fine 1995-96 season at Villa. He joined the club in 1990 as a teenager and has come of age at Villa Park. Born 3-12-71.

ANDY TOWNSEND: Republic of Ireland midfielder bought for £2.1 million in 1993. Born 23-7-63.

RAY HOUGHTON: Born in Scotland but an experienced Irish international. Joined Villa in 1992 after five seasons with Liverpool but left for Crystal Palace in 1995. Born 9-1-62.

STEVE STAUNTON: Another Irish international and ex-Liverpool player. Joined Aston Villa in 1991. He was ever-present in the successful 1992-93 Villa side. Born 19-1-69.

GARETH SOUTHGATE: Watford-born defender signed in 1995 from his first club Crystal Palace for £2.5 million. Has fought his way into the England squad. Born 3-9-70.

MARK DRAPER: Midfielder who made over 400 appearances for Notts County before joining Leicester in 1994. After one year at Filbert Street, he signed for Aston Villa for £3.25 million, where he has made an immediate impact. Born 11-11-70.

Colin Hendry

Tim Sherwood

1992-93

PRE-SEASON: Having set the pace in the old Second Division in the previous season, Blackburn stumble badly towards the end and win promotion via the play-offs, beating Leicester 1-0 at Wembley thanks to a Mike Newell penalty. It is Blackburn's first play-off success in four attempts.

THE SEASON: Blackburn's season begins with a 3-3 draw at Crystal Palace, Stuart Ripley scoring Blackburn's first goal and Alan Shearer adding the other two.

It proves to be the start to a successful campaign which includes home and away wins over Arsenal and home victories over Liverpool, Leeds and Aston Villa.

Shearer proves himself an expert goalscorer with 16 in the Premier League, while partner Mike Newell finds the target 12 times. The club also benefits from a high number of own goals – four.

The season ends with Blackburn in a highly-impressive fourth place.

Best win 7-1 defeat of Norwich at home in early October; worst defeat 5-2 at Leeds in April. Top scorer: Alan Shearer (16).

1993-94

PRE-SEASON: Having enjoyed a successful return to the top flight, Blackburn are happy to watch the blending of their expensively-acquired squad, Alan Shearer (£3.3 million in July 1992), Paul Warhurst (£2.7 million in September 1993), Kevin Gallacher (£2.5 million in March 1993) and Tim Flowers (£2 million in November 1993).

Blackburn Rovers facts and figures

CLUB ADDRESS: Ewood Park, Blackburn, Lancashire BB2 4JF.

TELEPHONE: 01254-698888

FAX: 01254-671042

CLUBCALL: 0891 121179

The club was formed in 1875, turning professional in 1880.

PREVIOUS GROUNDS: In 1875-76 the club was a nomad side, in 1876 home matches were played at Oozehead Ground, 1877 Pleasington Cricket Ground, 1878 Alexandra Meadows, 1881 Leamington Road, 1890 Ewood Park.

RECORD ATTENDANCE: 61,783 v Bolton Wanderers, FA Cup 6th rnd, March 1929.

BIGGEST WIN: 11-0 v Rossendale, FA Cup 1st rnd, October 1884.

BIGGEST DEFEAT: 0-8 v Arsenal, Div 1, February 1933.

TOP LEAGUE SCORER IN A SEASON: Ted Harper (43), 1925-26.

HIGHEST AGGREGATE SCORER: Simon Garner (168), 1978-92.

MOST CAPPED PLAYER: Bob Crompton (41) for England.

STARS OF YESTERYEAR: Bobby Langton (1946-47 and 1953-55), Bill Eckersley (1947-60), Ronnie Clayton (1950-68), Bryan Douglas (1954-68), Andy McEvoy (1958-66), Simon Garner (1978-92).

GREAT MANAGERS: Thomas Mitchell (1884-96), Jack Marshall (1960-67), Howard Kendall (1979-81), Kenny Dalglish (1991-95).

HONOURS: 1884 – FA Cup winners, 1885 – FA Cup winners, 1886 – FA Cup winners, 1890 – FA Cup winners, 1891 – FA Cup winners, 1911-12 – First Division champions, 1913-14 – First Division champions, 1928 – FA Cup winners, 1938-39 – Second Division champions, 1974-75 – Third Division champions, 1994-95 – Premier League champions.

THE SEASON: A 2-1 opening away win at Chelsea is followed by a 3-2 home defeat at the hands of Norwich City. This is a remarkable result given that, over the course of the season, Blackburn are to concede only eight more goals at home.

They win 13 succesive home matches and take four points from Manchester United – the eventual champions and FA Cup winners.

Shearer scores 31 goals, including one hat-trick, as Blackburn finish the season in second place, eight points behind United.

Best wins both 3-0 away, at Everton and home to Wimbledon; worst defeat ironically by Wimbledon six weeks later by 4-1. Top scorer: Alan Shearer (31).

1994-95

PRE-SEASON: The club pay Norwich City £5 million for Chris Sutton in July 1994, beating off the challenge of Arsenal and Manchester United. Sutton, converted from a defender into a striker by Norwich, had been a prolific scorer for the East Anglia club.

As Premiership runners-up, Blackburn take on double-winners Manchester United in the Charity Shield and lose 2-0.

THE SEASON: A 1-1 draw at Southampton sets off the season for Blackburn, who enjoy an impressive home run, winning 17 out of 21 matches and drawing two.

They are beaten home and away by Manchester United, and the low point comes in the Uefa Cup when they are defeated by Swedish part-timers Trelleborg, drawing 2-2 away and losing 1-0 at home. Apart from that, it is sunshine most of the way.

Shearer scores 34 Premiership goals and Sutton 15 as the two form a Championship understanding which falters in the last few weeks with a home defeat by lowly Manchester City and successive away reverses to West Ham and Liverpool. But Blackburn just hold their nerve to take the title by one point from Manchester United.

Best win 4-0 at home to Coventry in August; worst defeat 3-1 at Tottenham in February. Top scorer: Alan Shearer (34).

1995-96

PRE-SEASON: Manager Kenny Dalglish moves upstairs to become technical director and assistant Ray Harford is promoted to team manager.

THE SEASON: The defending champions make a slow start following an opening day 1-0 victory over QPR.

Successive 2-1 defeats at the hands of Sheffield Wednesday, Bolton and Manchester United mean they are soon off the pace and they do not win a second Premiership match until late September when they demolish Coventry 5-1.

Their European Cup campaign falls flat and they win just one of the group matches, beating Rosenberg 4-1.

Graeme Le Saux breaks a leg in December and misses the rest of the season. Chris Coleman joins from Crystal Palace for £2.8 million in December and Garry Flitcroft comes from Manchester City late in the season.

Blackburn beat Nottingham Forest 7-0 at home and 5-1 at the City ground but inconsistent early-season form prevents their qualifying for Europe in spite of finishing the season with a 3-2 win at Chelsea.

Best win 7-0 at home to Nottingham Forest; worst defeat 5-0 at Coventry City. Top scorer: Alan Shearer (31)

THE MANAGERS: Kenny Dalglish 1991-95, Ray Harford 1995- .

Mark Hughes

Dennis Wise

1992-93

PRE-SEASON: Ian Porterfield adds experience to his squad with the purchase of Mal Donaghy, for £150,000, and Mick Harford, for £300,000. He also buys Norwich striker Robert Fleck for £2.1 million.

THE SEASON: Chelsea's introduction to the Premier League is not impressive, as they fail to win in their first four games. Things then improve and, with the help of eight goals from Harford, they begin December in fourth place.

Twelve games then follow without another win and they drop to 11th place. Ian Porterfield loses his job and David Webb is put in charge until the end of the season.

They reach their lowest position of 15th in March but the emergence of Neil Shipperley and the return to form of Tony Cascarino helps them to a final place of 11th. They finish the season with 56 points, having drawn 14 of their 42 fixtures and showing no consistency.

Best win 4-0 v Middlesbrough in April; worst defeats 4-2 disappointments at Manchester City and Sheffield United. Top scorer: Mick Harford (9).

1993-94

PRE-SEASON: England favourite Glenn Hoddle takes over as player-manager, whetting the appetites of fans of skilful football. He sells Andy Townsend to Villa for £2 million and buys Gavin Peacock from Newcastle for £1.25 million.

THE SEASON: Chelsea's disappointing first Premier season is not improved upon as they win only one of their first six games, though the form of Gavin Peacock is encouraging. They then have a run of 11 games at the end of the

Chelsea facts and figures

CLUB ADDRESS: Stamford Bridge, London SW6 1HS.

TELEPHONE: 0171-385 5545

FAX: 0171-381 4831

CLUBCALL: 0891-121159

The club was formed in 1905, turning professional in the same year.

RECORD ATTENDANCE: 82,905 v Arsenal, Div 1, October 1935.

BIGGEST WIN: 13-0 v Jeunesse Hautcharage, European Cup-Winners Cup, September 1971.

BIGGEST DEFEAT: 1-8 v Wolverhampton Wanderers, Div 1, September 1953.

TOP LEAGUE SCORER IN A SEASON: Jimmy Greaves (41), 1960-61.

HIGHEST AGGREGATE SCORER: Bobby Tambling (164), 1958-70.

MOST CAPPED PLAYER: Ray Wilkins (24) for England.

STARS OF YESTERYEAR: Hughie Gallacher (1930-34), Jimmy Greaves (1957-61), Peter Bonetti (1959-78), Bobby Tambling (1959-70), Terry Venables (1960-66), Ron Harris (1961-80), Peter Osgood (1964-74), Ray Wilkins (1973-79).

GREAT MANAGERS: Billy Birrell (1939-52), Ted Drake (1952-61), Tommy Docherty (1962-67), Dave Sexton (1967-74).

HONOURS: 1954-55 – First Division champions,
1964-65 – League Cup winners,
1969-70 – FA Cup winners,
1970-71 – European Cup-Winners' Cup winners,
1983-84 – Second Division champions,
1988-89 – Second Division champions.

year without a victory, slumping to 21st in the table and looking like an early candidate for relegation.

The arrival of Mark Stein, from Stoke, sees an improvement as he scores 11 goals in nine games, making him Chelsea's highest scorer for the season. John Spencer is also in good striking form and the Blues settle into 14th position from the beginning of April to the end of the season. Their home record is quite impressive but they end with only 51 points, having won a mere two games away from Stamford Bridge.

Best win 4-2 against Everton; worst defeat 4-1 at Leeds. Top scorer: Mark Stein (13).

1994-95

PRE-SEASON: Glenn Hoddle ends David Rocastle's unhappy period at Manchester City by bringing him to Stamford Bridge for £1.25 million and Paul Furlong arrives from Watford.

THE SEASON: The forward line of Spencer, Peacock and Furlong begins the season well with wins in their first three games, all three hitting the net. But again, Chelsea fail to reach any form of consistency and end November in eighth place.

Ten games without a victory sees them slump to 13th, but Stein once again forces his way into the team by his goalscoring. Still the Blues fail to rise any higher than 11th as the goals, plentiful at the beginning of the season, dry up.

The top scorer for the season is Spencer with 11 goals, one more than Furlong. Craig Burley and Scott Minto break into the senior side while Shipperley departs for Southampton and Wise has off-field troubles.

Chelsea finish the season with 54 points, having won only seven games at Stamford Bridge, a reversal of the form of the previous year.

Best win 4-0 v Leicester in October; worst defeat 4-2 at Newcastle. Top scorer: John Spencer (11).

1995-96

PRE-SEASON: Mark Hughes is signed from Manchester United for £1.5 million and Ruud Gullit comes on a free transfer from Sampdoria.

THE SEASON: A slow start improves in September with a 3-1 win at West Ham followed by a 3-0 home victory over Southampton.

Chelsea, however, promise much without putting together a run of results and boardroom bickering between long-serving chairman Ken Bates and director Matthew Harding.

The two patch up their differences, and prompted by Gullit, Chelsea play some impressive football. Dan Petrescu joins for £2.3 million from Sheffield Wednesday.

They reach the FA Cup semi-final but despite taking the lead, lose 2-1 to Manchester United. The season ends with manager Glenn Hoddle accepting the England coaching job, with Gullit taking over as player/manager.

Best win 5-0 at home to Middlesbrough in February; worst defeat 4-1 at home to Manchester United. Top scorer: John Spencer (13).

THE MANAGERS: Ian Porterfield 1991-93, David Webb 1993, Glenn Hoddle 1993-96, Ruud Gullit 1996- .

Steve Ogrizovic

Dion Dublin

1992-93

PRE-SEASON: Managerial musical chairs at Highfield Road. Bobby Gould returns to the club as joint manager with Don Howe, Howe resigns because of travel problems and Phil Neal takes over as Gould's assistant. On the playing side Phil Babb and John Williams come in, Paul Furlong and Kevin Drinkell leave.

THE SEASON: Coventry are at their inconsistent best, winning six of their first eight Premier matches, but crashing out of the League Cup to Third Division Scarborough.

Gould steals goal machine Mick Quinn away from Newcastle for £250,000 in December. Quinn hits the net 10 times in his first six matches.

City slump at the end of the season finishing 15th with 52 points, three points above relegated Crystal Palace. They lose 10 matches at Highfield Road.

Best win 5-1 thrashing of Liverpool in December; worst defeat 5-0 at champions-to-be Manchester Utd nine days later. Top scorer: Mick Quinn (17).

1993-94

PRE-SEASON: City lose defender Andy Pearce to Sheffield Wednesday for £500,000. Veteran striker Mick Harford is a surprise signing.

THE SEASON: On the pitch, Coventry enjoy a stable season. Off it, they are rocked by the resignation of Bobby Gould just ten minutes after a 5-1 defeat at QPR. Phil Neal takes over.

Discovery of the season is Zimbabwean striker Peter Ndlovu, who assumes the goalscoring responsibility from the out-of-form Quinn.

Coventry City facts and figures

CLUB ADDRESS: Highfield Road Stadium, King Richard Street, Coventry CV2 4FW

TELEPHONE: 01203 223535

FAX: 01203 630318

CLUBLINE: 0891 121166

The club was formed in 1883, turning professional in 1893.

PREVIOUS GROUNDS: Binley Road and Stoke Road.

RECORD ATTENDANCE: 51,455 v Wolverhampton Wanderers, Div 2, April 1967.

BIGGEST WIN: 9-0 v Bristol City, Div 3 South, April 1934.

BIGGEST DEFEATS: 2-11 v Berwick Rangers, FA Cup, November 1901 and 2-10 v Norwich, Div 3 South, March 1930.

TOP LEAGUE SCORER IN A SEASON: Clarrie Bourton (49), 1931-32.

HIGHEST AGGREGATE SCORER: Clarrie Bourton (171), 1931-37.

MOST CAPPED PLAYER: Dave Clements 21 (48) for N. Ireland and Ronnie Rees 21 (39) for Wales.

STARS OF YESTERYEAR: Clarrie Bourton (1931-37), Reg Matthews (1950-56), George Curtis (1956-70), Ronnie Rees (1962-67), Bill Glazier (1964-75), Mick Coop (1966-80), Ernie Hunt (1967-73), Willie Carr (1967-74), Denis Mortimer (1969-75), Ian Wallace (1976-80), Mark Hateley (1978-83), Kevin Gallacher (1990-93), Phil Babb (1992-94).

GREAT MANAGERS: Harry Storer (1931-45 and 1948-53), Jimmy Hill (1961-67), Noel Cantwell (1968-72), Gordon Milne (1974-81), John Sillett (1987-90).

HONOURS: 1935-36 – Third Division (South) champions, 1963-64 – Third Division champions, 1966-67 – Second Division champions, 1986-87 – FA Cup winners.

Coventry finish in 11th position with 56 points. Their 42 Premiership games contain just 88 goals.

Best win 4-0 against Manchester City in February; worst defeat 5-1 at QPR. Top scorer: Peter Ndlovu (11).

1994-95

PRE-SEASON: American World Cup star Cobi Jones arrives at Highfield Road for £300,000. Wolves midfielder Paul Cook joins him just three days before the season kicks off.

THE SEASON: Coventry fans fear the worst as their team's first two away trips end in 4-0 defeats at Newcastle and Blackburn.

In the space of seven days in September, the club receives a record fee as £3.6 million Phil Babb moves to Liverpool, and then pays out a record £2 million to Manchester Utd for Dion Dublin.

Despite a mid-season revival, City slip back into the bottom three in February. Neal pays the price with his job.

The new manager is Ron Atkinson, just three months after being sacked by Aston Villa. Big Ron works the miracle and Coventry avoid the drop. He buys Kevin Richardson from Villa and immediately makes him club captain. They finish 16th with 50 points, having scored just 44 goals.

Best win 4-2 against relegation-bound Leicester; worst defeat 5-1 Christmas stuffing at Sheffield Wednesday. Top scorer: Dion Dublin (16).

1995-96

PRE-SEASON: Atkinson bids to transform Coventry from a team of perennial strugglers into contenders for a place in Europe. He buys midfielders Marques Isaias, Paul Telfer and John Salako for a combined £3.15 million.

THE SEASON: Despite further big-name purchases, City spend all season battling to avoid relegation, only preserving their top-flight status with a final day 0-0 draw with Leeds.

Coventry become one of the Premiership's top-spending clubs as they splash out £7 million to bring Noel Whelan, Richard Shaw, Eoin Jess and Liam Daish to Highfield Road. A leaky defence concedes 60 goals but tightens up just in time with successive clean sheets in the last three games. Coventry finish in 16th position, level on 38 points with Manchester City who go down.

Best win 5-0 hammering of Blackburn in December, avenging their worst defeat 5-1 at the hands of the champions in September. Top scorer: Dion Dublin (16).

THE MANAGERS: Bobby Gould 1992-93, Phil Neal 1993-95, Ron Atkinson 1995-

Noel Whelan

Marco Gabbiadini

1992-93

PRE-SEASON: Armed with Lionel Pickering's millions, manager Arthur Cox looks forward to emulating Kenny Dalglish's success at Blackburn by leading Derby into the Premier League.

THE SEASON: Cox reacts to Derby's disastrous start by signing defensive colossus Craig Short for a club record £2.5 million from Notts County.

The team hits form away from the Baseball Ground, winning seven consecutive matches, but it is a different story at home, where they lose ten League games.

Derby reach the quarter-finals of the FA Cup and the final of the Anglo-Italian. However, it is no compensation for eighth position in Division 1. Derby's 66 points are ten short of the play-offs.

Best win 7-0 thrashing of Southend in the Coca-Cola Cup in October; worst defeat 3-0 at Portsmouth in April. Top scorer: Paul Kitson (23).

1993-94

PRE-SEASON: Cox continues to strengthen Derby's squad as he signs Gary Charles from Nottingham Forest and Sheffield Wednesday's American midfielder John Harkes.

THE SEASON: Despite an opening day 5-0 win over Sunderland, their best start for 79 years, Derby again under-achieve.

Cox resigns in October, citing persistent back trouble as the reason. His assistant Roy McFarland takes over.

Derby rarely threaten automatic promotion. They finish fourth with 71

Derby County facts and figures

CLUB ADDRESS: Baseball Ground, Shaftesbury Crescent, Derby DE3 8NB.

TELEPHONE: 01332 340105

FAX: 01332 293514

CLUBLINE: 0891 121187

The club was formed in 1884, turning professional the same year.

PREVIOUS GROUND: Racecourse Ground.

The club has been called Derby County since its foundation.

RECORD ATTENDANCE: 41,826 v Tottenham, Div 1, September 1969.

BIGGEST WIN: 12-0 v Finn Harps, Uefa Cup 1st Rnd, September 1976.

BIGGEST DEFEAT: 2-11 v Everton, FA Cup 1st Rnd, 1889-90.

TOP LEAGUE SCORER IN A SEASON: Jack Bowers (37), 1930-31, Ray Straw (37), 1956-57.

HIGHEST AGGREGATE SCORER: Steve Bloomer (293), 1892-1906 and 1910-14.

MOST CAPPED PLAYER: Peter Shilton 34 (125) for England.

STARS OF YESTERYEAR: Steve Bloomer (1892-1906 and 1910-14), Tommy Cooper (1925-34), Peter Doherty (1945-46), Raich Carter (1945-48), Kevin Hector (1966-78 and 1980-82), John O'Hare (1967-74), Roy McFarland (1967-80), Dave Mackay (1968-70), Archie Gemmill (1970-77), Colin Todd (1971-78).

GREAT MANAGERS: Jimmy Methven (1906-22), Harry Storer (1955-62), Brian Clough (1967-73), Dave Mackay (1973-76).

HONOURS: 1911-12, 1914-15 – Division 2 champions, 1945-46 – FA Cup winners, 1956-57 – Division 3 North champions, 1968-69 – Division 2 champions, 1971-72, 1974-75 – Division 1 champions, 1986-87 – Division 2 champions.

Jim Smith celebrates a return to the top flight

GARY CHARLES: Former England international (2 caps) signed from Nottm Forest. He moved with Tommy Johnson to Aston Villa in a £2.9 million deal in January 1995. Born 13-4-70.

IGOR STIMAC: Captain of Croatia, who signed from Hadjuk Split in October 1995 for £1.5 million. Scored on his Derby debut in a 5-1 victory over Tranmere. Born 6-9-67.

CRAIG SHORT: Derby's record signing when he joined for £2.5 million from Notts County in September 1992. Joined Everton for £2.4 million in July 1995. Born 25-6-68.

MARK PEMBRIDGE: Scored 16 goals in his first season with Derby after joining them from Luton in May 1992. Moved to Sheffield Wednesday at the start of the 1995-96 season for £900,000. Born 29-11-70.

ROBIN VAN DER LAAN: Dutch midfielder who was a driving force behind Derby's promotion. Made captain after moving for £475,000 in July 1995 from Port Vale. Born 5-9-68.

DARRYL POWELL: Signed from Portsmouth for £750,000 in July 1995. Forms a dynamic midfield partnership with Van Der Laan. Born 15-1-71.

MARCO GABBIADINI: Prolific scorer for Derby since his £1.2 million move from Crystal Palace in January 1992. Made his name at York and Sunderland. Born 20-1-68.

TOMMY JOHNSON: Moved to Aston Villa in a combined £2.9 million deal with Gary Charles in January 1995. Spent almost three years at the Baseball Ground. Born 15-1-71.

PAUL KITSON: Derby's top scorer in his first full season after signing from Leicester. Moved to Newcastle for £2.25 million in September 1994. Born 9-1-71.

DEAN STURRIDGE: Product of the Derby youth system who was the find of the 1994-95 promotion campaign. Born 26-7-73.

---

points and then suffer the heartache of losing 2-1 to Midlands rivals Leicester in the play-off final at Wembley.

Best win the opening day 5-0 success at Sunderland; worst defeats 4-0 flops against Wolves and Tranmere. Top scorers: Marco Gabbiadini and Tommy Johnson (15).

1994-95

PRE-SEASON: Lionel Pickering decides enough is enough and puts his cheque book away. In a pivotal move for the club's future, Roy McFarland is told to succeed or else.

THE SEASON: The chairman's patience is tested further by a return of just one point from the first four matches. He decides it is time to sell.

Paul Kitson moves to Newcastle for £2.25 million, Tommy Johnson and Gary Charles leave for Aston Villa in a combined £2.9 million deal.

With Derby wallowing in mid-table, Roy McFarland is sacked in April. Despite a late surge, County finish ninth with 66 points but without a manager.

Best win 5-0 hammering of play-off bound Tranmere in April; worst defeat 4-1 at Millwall in August. Top scorer: Marco Gabbiadini (13).

1995-96

PRE-SEASON: New manager Jim Smith has to cope with losing club captain Craig Short to Everton for £2.4 million, but moves to pick up midfielders Robin van der Laan and Darryl Powell from Port Vale and Portsmouth respectively.

THE SEASON: Smith brings all of his considerable experience to bear as he steers Derby back to the top flight after a five-year absence.

It looks far from promising early in November, though, with the Rams languishing in 17th place after a 5-1 thrashing at Tranmere.

Incredibly, Derby are eight points clear at the top by January following a run of 10 wins in 11 games.

But the chasing pack, especially Sunderland and Crystal Palace, catch up. Derby need to beat Palace in their penultimate match to assure themselves of promotion. They do, 2-1, and finish as runners-up with 79 points.

Best win 6-2 on Easter Monday against Tranmere avenging their worst defeat, 5-1 at Tranmere in November. Top scorer: Dean Sturridge (20).

THE MANAGERS: Arthur Cox 1984-93, Roy McFarland 1993-95, Jim Smith 1995-

Neville Southall

Andrei Kanchelskis

EVERTON
– The Premiership History

1992-93 PRE-SEASON: In July the club reveals it has debts of £3.6 million but still spends £500,000 in bringing Paul Rideout to the attack from Glasgow Rangers.

THE SEASON: A good start – a 1-1 home draw with Sheffield Wednesday, Barry Horne scoring the club's first-ever Premier League goal, is followed by a stunning 3-0 win at Manchester United – the eventual champions.

But the season hits a trough and the club go through six home matches without a victory. Away form is not much better.

Everton are left hovering around the relegation area and while never in serious danger they are not that far away from trouble. They end the season 13th.

Best win 5-2 at Manchester City; worst defeat was 5-3 at home to QPR. Top scorer: Tony Cottee (12).

1993-94 PRE-SEASON: Peter Beardsley has gone to Newcastle but Everton take Graham Stuart from Chelsea for £850,000.

THE SEASON: Another flying start for Everton sees them win at Southampton, 2-0, then at home to Manchester City and Sheffield United and in the first published Premiership table of the season Everton are second behind Liverpool.

Everton facts and figures

CLUB ADDRESS: Goodison Park, Liverpool L4 4EL.

TELEPHONE: 0151-521 2020

FAX: 0151-523 9666

CLUBCALL: 0891-121199

The club was formed in 1878, turning professional in 1885.

PREVIOUS GROUNDS: 1878 Stanley Park, 1882 Priory Road, 1884 Anfield Road, 1892 Goodison Park.

RECORD ATTENDANCE: 78,299 v Liverpool – Div 1, September 1948.

BIGGEST WIN: 11-2 v Derby County – FA Cup 1st rnd, January 1890.

BIGGEST DEFEAT: 4-10 v Tottenham Hotspur – Div 1, October 1958.

TOP LEAGUE SCORER IN A SEASON: William "Dixie" Dean (60), 1927-28.

HIGHEST AGGREGATE SCORER: William "Dixie" Dean (349) – 1925-37.

MOST CAPPED PLAYER: Neville Southall (85 at end of March 1996) for Wales.

STARS OF YESTERYEAR: William "Dixie" Dean (1925-37), Tommy Lawton (1936-39), Ted Sagar (1929-52), Brian Labone (1957-71), Bobby Collins (1959-62), Alex Young (1960-67), Alan Ball (1966-71), Joe Royle (1965-74) Bob Latchford (1973-81), Andy Gray (1983-85), Gary Lineker (85-86).

GREAT MANAGERS: William Cuff (1901-18), Thomas McIntosh (1919-35), Theo Kelly (1936-48), Cliff Britton (1948-56), Harry Catterick (1961-73), Howard Kendall (1981-87 & 1990-93).

HONOURS: 1890-91 – First Division champions,
1906 – FA Cup winners,
1914-15 – First Division champions,
1927-28 – First Division champions,
1930-31 – Second Division champions,
1931-32 – First Division champions,
1933 – FA Cup winners,
1938-39 – First Division champions,
1962-63 – First Division champions,
1966 – FA Cup winners,
1969-70 – First Division champions,
1984 – FA Cup winners,
1984-85 – First Division champions, European Cup Winners' Cup winners,
1986-87 – First Division champions,
1995 – FA Cup winners.

Tony Cottee, the club's leading scorer the previous season, is again top marksman, but with only 16 goals.

The next best is Paul Rideout with six and a lack of goals along with a mid-season slump makes it a long uphill battle for the club.

Everton play their last match of the season needing to win to avoid relegation. After 20 minutes of that match – at home to Wimbledon – they are trailing 2-0, yet stage a great comeback to win 3-2 and stay in the Premiership, finishing 17th.

Best win 6-2 v Swindon in January; worst defeat 5-1 by Norwich at Goodison Park in September. Top scorer: Tony Cottee (16).

1994-95

PRE-SEASON: Mike Walker, the former Norwich manager, spends heavily, bringing in Vinny Samways from Tottenham for £2.2 million and then Daniel Amokachi, from Bruges, for £3 million. Tony Cottee is allowed to return to West Ham in part-exchange for David Burrows.

THE SEASON: This time there is not even a good start to the season. An opening day 2-2 draw at home to Aston Villa is followed by four successive defeats. It takes Everton 13 Premiership matches to record a first win – a 1-0 home victory over West Ham.

By that time they had been dumped out of the Coca-Cola Cup by lower division Portsmouth.

Walker is fired in mid-November and Joe Royle, former Goodison playing hero and manager at Oldham for over ten years, makes a triumphant return.

Liverpool are beaten in his first match in charge, results improve and while the club hover near the relegation zone they escape that fate more comfortably than in the previous year. Duncan Ferguson joins the club initially on loan from Rangers.

For good measure a dazzling FA Cup run takes them to Wembley where Paul Rideout's goal is enough for them to beat favourites Manchester United 1-0.

Best win 4-1 at home to Ipswich Town in December; worst defeat 4-0 at Manchester City in August. Top scorer: Paul Rideout (13).

1995-96

PRE-SEASON: The FA Cup holders make one major pre-season purchase, Andrei Kanchelskis bought from Manchester United for £5 million in a drawn-out saga.

THE SEASON: A 1-0 Charity Shield win does not set Everton up for the greatest of season – but it is a vast improvement on recent years. They lose the first home match 2-0 to Arsenal but after some patchy performances hit a six-match unbeaten run in November.

Duncan Ferguson receives a jail sentence for an assault on an opponent, relating back to his days in Scotland, but has a lengthy playing ban overturned.

The highlight of the season is a 2-1 win at Liverpool in November and they finish with four victories out of six but results go against them in the final day of the season and they miss out on a Uefa Cup place.

Neville Southall is an ever-present. The club lose in the European Cup Winners' Cup second round to the Dutch side Feyenoord.

Best win 4-0 at home to Middlesbrough; worst defeat 3-1 at home to Newcastle in October and away to QPR in April. Top scorer: Andrei Kanchelskis (16).

THE MANAGERS: Howard Kendall 1990-93, Mike Walker 1994, Joe Royle 1994-

Gary McAllister

Tony Yeboah

1992-93

PRE-SEASON: After winning the championship in the previous season Leeds supporters are optimistic for the first Premier season. Howard Wilkinson buys Scott Sellars for £950,000 and David Rocastle for £2 million. Neither player settles at Elland Road.

THE SEASON: The first Premier game is encouraging, a 2-1 victory over Wimbledon at Elland Road, thanks to a brace from Lee Chapman. Home form continues to be impressive and Cantona and Chapman continue to score consistently.

Away from home the story is different. Heavy defeats at Ipswich, Manchester City and Middlesbrough see them languishing at the lower end of the table. In November Wilkinson outrages fans by selling Eric Cantona to Manchester United for £1,200,000. He does not replace him.

They record no wins away from home, conceding 45 goals and scoring only 17. Their home form is tremendous, losing only one game, but they end the season on only 51 points.

Best win 5-0 v Tottenham in August; worst defeat 0-4 at Manchester City and at Tottenham. Top scorer: Lee Chapman (15).

1993-94

PRE-SEASON: Wilkinson sells his top scorer, Lee Chapman, to Portsmouth for only £250,000 and buys Brian Deane from Sheffield United for £2.7 million.

THE SEASON: Leeds fail to win any of their first three away games and the curse of the previous season seems to be cast again. But Rod Wallace comes into the side and fortunes change. A run of 14 games without defeat, and Leeds' first away wins in the Premiership, see them climb to second.

Leeds United facts and figures

CLUB ADDRESS: Elland Road, Leeds LS11 0ES.

TELEPHONE: 0113-2716037

FAX: 0113-2720370

CLUBCALL: 0891-121181

The club was formed in 1919, following the disbandonment of Leeds City, turning professional in 1920.

RECORD ATTENDANCE: 57,892 v Sunderland – FA Cup 5th rnd replay, March 1967.

BIGGEST WIN: 10-0 v Lyn (Oslo) in European Cup, September 1969.

BIGGEST DEFEAT: 1-8 v Stoke City in Div 1, August 1934.

TOP LEAGUE SCORER IN A SEASON: John Charles (42), 1953-54.

HIGHEST AGGREGATE SCORER: Peter Lorimer (168), 1965-79 and 1983-86.

MOST CAPPED PLAYER: Billy Bremner (54), 1959-76 for Scotland.

STARS OF YESTERYEAR: John Charles (1948-56 and 1962), Jack Charlton (1952-72), Billy Bremner (1959-76), Norman Hunter (1961-76), Johnny Giles (1963-74), Gordon Strachan (1989-95).

GREAT MANAGERS: Don Revie (1961-74), Howard Wilkinson (1988-).

HONOURS: 1923-24 – Second Division champions, 1963-64 – Second Division champions, 1967-68 – League Cup winners, European Fairs Cup winners, 1968-69 – First Division champions, 1970-71 – European Fairs Cup winners, 1971-72 – FA Cup winners, 1973-74 - First Division champions, 1989-90 – Second Division champions, 1991-92 – First Division champions.

In October David Batty is sold to Blackburn for £2.7 million and December sees the arrival of David White from Manchester City in a player-exchange deal for David Rocastle. Rod Wallace is out for four games at the beginning of 1994 and the goals dry up. They drop to fifth, where they stay until the end of the season.

Leeds finish the season with an impressive 70 points, but are still 22 points behind Manchester United. They win only five games away from home, which prevents them challenging for leadership.

Best win 5-0 v Swindon in the last game of the season; worst defeat 4-0 at home to Norwich. Top scorer: Rod Wallace (17).

1994-95
PRE-SEASON: Wilkinson invests in Carlton Palmer for £2.6 million and South African Phil Masinga for £275,000. He also buys veteran Nigel Worthington as cover for the injured Tony Dorigo.

THE SEASON: 1994-95 begins slowly with a 0-0 draw at Upton Park and then youngster Noel Whelan begins to impress, scoring six times in eleven games. This leaves Leeds in sixth, with a prolific scoring partnership between Deane and Whelan starting to develop.

But four games over the Christmas period produce no goals for Leeds. Whelan loses his place to Tony Yeboah, a Ghanaian bought for £3.4 million. He soon justifies his price tag, scoring 12 times in the remainder of the season, to end as Leeds' top scorer.

His goals help lift the side to fifth again, the position they occupied the previous season. They finish with 73 points, again out of contention with the leaders. Again, less than impressive away form prevents them climbing any higher.

Best wins 4-0 over QPR and Ipswich; worst defeats 0-3 at Everton and Nottingham Forest. Top scorer: Tony Yeboah (12).

1995-96
PRE-SEASON: Leeds stick with their tried and tested squad and hope that Ghanaian Tony Yeboah can give them a vital cutting edge.

THE SEASON: Leeds make a sprint start to the season, winning 2-1 at West Ham then beating Liverpool 1-0 thanks to a stunning goal from Tony Yeboah.

They remain in a challenging position for the early part of the season in spite of an 8-3 aggregate defeat in the Uefa Cup at the hands of PSV Eindhoven.

Leeds make good progress in the Coca-Cola Cup but are comprehensively beaten 3-0 by Aston Villa in the final.

Richard Jobson is signed for £1 million from Oldham in late October and Thomas Brolin comes from Parma for £4.5 million in November but as the season winds down, Leeds go into free fall losing six on the trot.

Chairman Leslie Silver steps down while manager Howard Wilkinson becomes the target of increasing hostility from the Elland Road fans.

Best win 4-2 at Wimbledon in September; worst defeats 6-2 at Sheffield Wednesday in December and 5-0 away at Liverpool. Top scorer: Tony Yeboah (12).

THE MANAGERS: Howard Wilkinson 1988-

Mark Robins

Garry Parker

1992-93

PRE-SEASON: Tommy Wright is sold to Middlesbrough for £650,000 in July, while Kevin Russell, Paul Reid and Ally Mauchlen also leave in Brian Little's summer clear-out. Colin Hill arrives at Filbert Street from Sheffield United in a £200,000 deal, and Little further strengthens his squad by signing Bobby Davison from Leeds.

THE SEASON: Leicester begin the Barclays League First Division season brightly by recording a 2-1 home win over Luton, but their form is patchy until January as they alternate wins with draws and defeats. The play-off push begins on February 28 with a 2-1 home victory over Birmingham. They win their next six games, with captain Steve Walsh providing the inspiration by scoring eight goals during this period.

Despite a shattering 7-1 defeat at Newcastle on the final day of the season, Little's men claim the final play-off spot. They overcome Portsmouth on aggregate in the semi-final, but slump to a 4-3 defeat against Swindon at Wembley to miss out on promotion.

Best win 5-2 at home to Watford; worst defeat 1-7 away to Newcastle. Top scorer: Steve Walsh (15).

1993-94

PRE-SEASON: David Speedie is enticed to Filbert Street on a free transfer from Southampton, signing a one-year contract with the promise of another year if Leicester are promoted. Brian Little adds Shaun Carey and Gavin Ward to his squad.

THE SEASON: City start the season well by losing only once in their first seven League matches. Speedie gives them an instant return on their investment by scoring seven goals in his first ten matches, and the signing of Iwan Roberts, in November, gives the Filbert Street strike force an extra boost.

Leicester City facts and figures

CLUB ADDRESS: Filbert Street, Leicester, LE2 7EL.

TELEPHONE: 0116-291 5000

FAX: 0116-247 0585

CLUBCALL: 0891 121185

The club was formed in 1884, and until 1919 it was called Leicester Fosse. The club turned professional in 1888.

PREVIOUS GROUNDS: Victoria Park 1884-87, Belgrave Road 1887, Victoria Park 1888-91.

RECORD ATTENDANCE: 47,298 v Tottenham Hotspur – FA Cup 5th round, February 18, 1928.

BIGGEST WIN: 10-0 v Portsmouth – Div 1, October 1928.

BIGGEST DEFEAT: 0-12 v Nottingham Forest – Div 1, April 1909.

TOP LEAGUE SCORER IN A SEASON: Arthur Rowley (44), 1956-57.

HIGHEST AGGREGATE SCORER: Arthur Chandler (273), 1923-34.

MOST CAPPED PLAYER: John O'Neill (39) for Northern Ireland.

STARS OF YESTERYEAR: Adam Black (1920-35), Arthur Chandler (1923-34), Arthur Rowley (1950-57), Gordon Banks (1959-66), Graham Cross (1960-76), Peter Shilton (1965-74), Gary Lineker (1978-85), John O'Neill (1978-1987), Alan Smith (1982-87), Gary McAllister (1985-90).

GREAT MANAGERS: William Orr (1926-32), Norman Bullock (1949-56), Matt Gillies (1959-68), Jock Wallace (1978-82), Gordon Milne (1982-86), David Pleat (1987-91), Brian Little (1991-94).

HONOURS: 1924-25 – Division 2 champions, 1936-37 – Division 2 champions, 1953-54 – Division 2 champions, 1956-57 – Division 2 champions, 1964 – League Cup winners, 1970-71 – Division 2 champions, 1979-80 – Division 2 champions.

Consecutive draws in their final three matches destroy any hopes Leicester have of automatic promotion, condemning them to the play-offs again. Goals from Speedie and Ian Ormondroyd give City a 2-1 aggregate win over Tranmere in the semi-final, setting up a Wembley meeting with Derby County.

Although Derby dominate most of the match, Steve Walsh ends his injury plagued season on a high note by netting the two goals which give Leicester a 2-1 win and a place in the Premiership.

Best win 4-0 at home to Millwall; worst defeat 0-4 away loss to Nottingham Forest. Top scorer: David Speedie (14).

1994-95

PRE-SEASON: Leicester prepare for the Premiership by signing talented midfielder Mark Draper from Notts County and Nicky Mohan from Middlesbrough.

THE SEASON: A 3-1 home defeat against Newcastle on opening day sets the tone for a disappointing year at Filbert Street. Despite the arrivals of Franz Carr and Mark Robins, Leicester fail to escape relegation.

Draper impresses with his consistency, but Leicester are dealt a body blow in December when Little walks out to become manager at Aston Villa, taking his coaching staff with him. Mark McGhee becomes the new manager, but five consecutive defeats in March kill hopes of survival.

Best win 3-1 at home to Tottenham; worst defeats are 0-4 away loss to Chelsea, while Manchester United beat them at home by the same score. Top scorer: Iwan Roberts (11).

1995-96

PRE-SEASON: Mark Draper leaves Filbert Street to join Aston Villa for a club record fee of £3.25 million in July. Gavin Ward, Nicky Mohan and Ian Ormondroyd are also transferred to Bradford for a combined £400,000, leaving a huge rebuilding job. McGhee looks abroad for new players, signing Australians Zeljko Kalac and Steve Corica. Scott Taylor joins from his old club Reading for £500,000.

THE SEASON: Leicester enjoy a superb start to the season by defeating eventual champions Sunderland 2-1, Mark Robins and new signing Corica scoring the goals, and lose only twice in their first 13 League matches.

City's form dips in November, and the club is suddenly thrown into crisis a month later when McGhee and his coaches walk out to take over at Wolves, almost a year after Brian Little left in similar fashion.

Martin O'Neill is the replacement manager, but his arrival does little to alter Leicester's indifferent form. The fans start to mount protests against the Filbert Street board, and Joachim joins Aston Villa in February for £1.5 million.

The signings of Steve Claridge, Neil Lennon and Julian Watts, plus the arrival of Muzzie Izzet on loan from Chelsea, spark Leicester's season back into life. Consecutive victories in their last four games win a play-off once more.

A Garry Parker goal defeats Stoke City in the semi-final, putting Leicester into a final with Crystal Palace. Although they fall behind early, a Parker penalty sends the match into extra time, allowing Claridge to seal promotion and a 2-1 win with almost the final kick of the match.

Best win 3-0 at home to Birmingham in the regular season's penultimate match; worst defeat 2-4 away to Ipswich. Top scorer: Iwan Roberts (20).

THE MANAGERS: Brian Little 1991-94, Mark McGhee 1994-95, Martin O'Neill 1995-

Stan Collymore

Robbie Fowler

1992-93

PRE-SEASON: Graeme Souness sells two of his more experienced players, Barry Venison and Ray Houghton, and pays £1 million to Watford for goalkeeper David James and £2.3 million to Tottenham for Paul Stewart.

THE SEASON: A mediocre season by Liverpool's standards begins with defeat at Nottingham Forest but then picks up with some good home wins, thanks to talented emerging players like Jamie Redknapp, Rob Jones and Steve McManaman.

Dean Saunders is sold to Villa in September and his place alongside Ian Rush is never filled. Rush finishes the season as highest scorer with 14 League goals. This season is Liverpool's year of young stars and the finishing position of sixth is impressive considering the inexperience of some of the team.

They amass 59 points in the season, let down by winning only three away games and conceding 37 goals away from Anfield.

Best win 5-0 v Crystal Palace in November; worst defeat 5-1 at Coventry. Top scorer: Ian Rush (14).

1993-94

PRE-SEASON: Souness strengthens his defence with Neil Ruddock, bought for £2.5 million from Spurs. He also buys Nigel Clough for £2,275,000 from Nottingham Forest but in the long run the England international does not settle.

THE SEASON: The year begins with Liverpool in commanding form, winning four of their opening five games, with Clough scoring four goals. This form slumps as they lose four consecutive games, scoring no goals.

Julian Dicks arrives from West Ham, where he would return a year later, for £1.5 million. Robbie Fowler is also given an opportunity in the team. He takes it, scoring 12 goals in the season to establish a regular place in the side.

In January Graeme Souness resigns, to be replaced by Roy Evans. He brings Ronnie Whelan back into the side and David James usurps Grobbelaar in goal.

Liverpool finish the season in eighth, again let down by their away form, losing 11 times away from Anfield.

Best win 5-0 v Swindon in August; worst defeat 3-0 at Newcastle. Top scorer: Ian Rush (14).

Liverpool facts and figures

CLUB ADDRESS: Anfield Road, Liverpool L4 0TH.
TELEPHONE: 0151-263-2361
FAX: 0151-260-8813
CLUBCALL: 0891-121184
The club was formed in 1892, turning professional the same year.
RECORD ATTENDANCE: 61,905 v Wolverhampton Wanderers – FA Cup 4th rnd, February 1952.
BIGGEST WIN: 11-0 v Stromsgodset Drammen – European Cup-Winners' Cup 1st rnd, September 1974.
BIGGEST DEFEAT: 1-9 v Birmingham City – Div 2, December 1954.
TOP LEAGUE SCORER IN SEASON: Roger Hunt (41), 1961-62.
HIGHEST AGGREGATE SCORER: Roger Hunt (245), 1959-69.
MOST CAPPED PLAYER: Ian Rush (75 to end of March 1996) for Wales.
STARS OF YESTERYEAR: Elisha Scott (1915-35), Billy Liddell (1946-61), Roger Hunt (1959-69), Ian St. John (1961-71), Ron Yeats (1961-71), Tommy Smith (1962-78), Emlyn Hughes (1966-78), Ray Clemence (1967-81), Kevin Keegan (1971-77), Ray Kennedy (1974-82), Kenny Dalglish (1977-85), Alan Hansen (1977-90), Graeme Souness (1978-84), Ronnie Whelan (1979-94), Ian Rush (1980-96), Peter Beardsley (1987-91).
GREAT MANAGERS: Bill Shankly (1959-74), Bob Paisley (1974-83), Kenny Dalglish (1985-91).

1994-95

PRE-SEASON: Liverpool's pre-season is disrupted as Mark Wright and Julian Dicks are left out of the squad to tour Germany for disciplinary reasons.

THE SEASON: Liverpool begin the season with an emphatic victory over Crystal Palace, winning 6-1. Fowler scores six goals in the first three games. Don Hutchison is sold to West Ham after off-field antics.

Fowler continues to show his class, hitting the net 25 times in the Premiership and ending second to Shearer in the league scoring tables.

Liverpool stay in the top five throughout the season, losing vital games against Ipswich and Coventry to prevent them challenging for the top of the table. The season sees the return of Walters, Wright and Thomas to the senior side to play alongside Redknapp and McManaman, who are now firmly established.

They end the season with 74 points, in fourth position.

Best win 6-1 v Crystal Palace in August; worst defeat 3-0 at West Ham. Top scorer: Robbie Fowler (25).

1995-96

PRE-SEASON: Liverpool smash the British transfer record when they sign Stan Collymore for £8.5 million from Nottingham Forest in mid-June.

THE SEASON: Four straight home wins suggest that Liverpool will be a major force again and Collymore marks his debut with the only goal of the match in the opening game against Sheffield Wednesday.

The first away trip is to Leeds where Liverpool lose to a wonder goal from Tony Yeboah. Home form is to remain impressive all season and the only defeat at Anfield is 2-1 by arch rivals Everton. Liverpool are knocked out of the Uefa Cup by the Danish side Brondby, having drawn 0-0 away but losing 1-0 at home. Two bad spells away from home cost Liverpool the chance to press for the championship as in November they take just one point from nine on their travels and then end the season with two defeats and three draws.

Liverpool enjoy a good FA Cup run, reaching the final after beating Aston Villa 3-0 in the semi-final, but they lose 1-0 to Manchester United in a drab Wembley finale to the season.

Best win 6-0 at home to Manchester City in October; worst defeats 2-1 at home to Everton, away at Newcastle and Middlesbrough. Top scorer: Robbie Fowler (28).

THE MANAGERS: Graeme Souness 1991-94, Roy Evans 1994-

HONOURS: 1893-94 – Second Division champions,
1895-96 – Second Division champions,
1900-01 – First Division champions,
1904-05 – Second Division champions,
1905-06 – First Division champions,
1921-22 – First Division champions,
1922-23 – First Division champions,
1946-47 – First Division champions,
1961-62 – Second Division champions,
1963-64 – First Division champions,
1964-65 – FA Cup winners,
1965-66 – First Division champions,
1972-73 – First Division champions, Uefa Cup winners,
1973-74 – FA Cup winners,
1975-76 – First Division champions, Uefa Cup winners,
1976-77 – First Division champions, European Cup winners,
1977-78 – European Cup winners,
1978-79 – First Division champions,
1979-80 – First Division champions,
1980-81 – League Cup winners, European Cup winners,
1981-82 – First Division champions,
League Cup winners,
1982-83 – First Division champions, League Cup winners,
1983-84 – First Division champions, League Cup winners, European Cup winners,
1985-86 – First Division champions, FA Cup winners,
1987-88 – First Division champions,
1988-89 – FA Cup winners,
1989-90 – First Division champions,
1991-92 – FA Cup winners,
1994-95 - League Cup winners.

Ryan Giggs

1992-93

PRE-SEASON: Peter Schmeichel is signed from Brondby for £550,000 while a testimonial for Sir Matt Busby attracts a crowd of over 33,000 and brings in £250,000. Bryan Robson is injured in a pre-season friendly.

THE SEASON: For a team that are to go on and take the first Premier League title, Manchester United make an appalling start to their campaign, losing 2-1 in their opening match at Sheffield United. They fare no better in their opening home game, losing 3-0 to Everton, but from there lose just four more times in the Premier League. The first win is at Southampton, 1-0 where Dion Dublin, a new signing, scores the only goal of the game.

The results improve at home but it is the signing of Eric Cantona – for £1.2 million from Leeds – which gives them the cutting edge. Cantona, a Championship winner with Leeds the previous season, scores nine goals for his new club as they romp away to take the title by ten points from Aston Villa.

Best win 5-0 v Coventry; worst defeat 0-3 at home to Everton in August. Top scorer: Mark Hughes (15).

1993-94

PRE-SEASON: Roy Keane at £3.75 million is the big summer signing from Nottingham Forest. Bryan Robson is sent off in friendly in South Africa against Arsenal but United gain revenge in the Charity Shield, winning 5-4 on penalties after a 1-1 draw.

THE SEASON: United are to dominate domestic football and achieve the Double. They start the season in style with a 2-0 win at Norwich City.

They are to lose four matches – twice to Chelsea who won at Old Trafford in September and then at Stamford Bridge in March. United's European Cup campaign is ended by Galatasaray, the Turkish champions.

At home, United power onwards and upwards, reaching the Coca-Cola Cup final where they are surprisingly beaten 3-1 by Aston Villa, managed by former United manager Ron Atkinson. The Premiership title is taken by a cosy 12 points, Blackburn coming second, and Chelsea are hammered 4-0 in the FA Cup final where Cantona scores two penalties.

Steve Bruce and Bryan Robson with the 1993-94 Premiership trophy

Manchester United facts and figures

CLUB ADDRESS: Old Trafford, Manchester M16 0RA.

TELEPHONE: 0161-872 1661

FAX: 0161-876 5502

CLUBCALL: 0891-121161

The club was formed in 1878, turning professional in 1902.

PREVIOUS GROUNDS: North Road and Monsall Road 1880-93, Bank Street 1893, Old Trafford 1910, Maine Road 1941-49.

RECORD ATTENDANCE: 70,504 v Aston Villa – Div 1, December 1920.

BIGGEST WIN: 10-0 v RS Anderlecht, European Cup, Prelim round, Sept 1956.

BIGGEST DEFEAT: 0-7 v Blackburn – Div 1, April 1926.

TOP LEAGUE SCORER IN SEASON: Dennis Viollet (32), 1959-60.

HIGHEST AGGREGATE SCORER: Bobby Charlton (198), 1956-73.

MOST CAPPED PLAYER: Bobby Charlton (106) for England.

STARS OF YESTERYEAR: Johnny Carey (1936-53), Jack Rowley (1946-54), Roger Byrne (1949-58), Billy Foulkes (1952-69), Tommy Taylor (1953-58), Duncan Edwards (1953-58), Bobby Charlton (1956-72), Nobby Stiles (1959-71), Denis Law (1962-72), Pat Crerand (1963-70), George

Best win 5-0 v Sheffield Wednesday; worst defeat 2-0 by Blackburn. Top scorer: Eric Cantona (18).

1994-95

PRE-SEASON: Manchester United pull out of the chase for Norwich's Chris Sutton – eventually bought by Blackburn. Paul Ince is told to sign a contract or leave the club – he eventually signs. Cantona is sent off in a pre-season friendly against Rangers at Ibrox. He scores a penalty in the 2-0 Charity Shield win at Wembley over Blackburn.

THE SEASON: Old Trafford is a fortress all fear to visit and where few prosper. Throughout the season United lose just one home match and concede only four goals. In fact, the first goal scored by a visiting side comes in the tenth Premiership game when Nottingham Forest win 2-1. Southampton and Leicester are the only other sides to score at Old Trafford.

United lose their title away from home, beaten at Leeds and Ipswich, and a ban for Eric Cantona, following a 'kung fu' attack on a fan at Crystal Palace, casts a shadow over their season. They lose the title by a point to Blackburn and are only that close because of Blackburn's late season stumble. United also lose the FA Cup final 1-0 to underdogs Everton.

Best win 9-0 v Ipswich in March; worst defeat 2-0 at Liverpool in March. Top scorer: Andrei Kanchelskis (14).

1995-96

PRE-SEASON: Manchester United become a selling club – Paul Ince, Andrei Kanchelskis and Mark Hughes all leave and Alex Ferguson turns to his youngsters – Gary and Philip Neville, Nicky Butt, Paul Scholes and David Beckham.

THE SEASON: That youth policy comes under immediate fire as a 3-1 opening defeat at the hands of Aston Villa suggests United may struggle.

It is not to be. The ship is immediately righted and they do not lose again in the Premiership until November, going down 1-0 at Arsenal.

They still trail Newcastle by seven points and a game more played in the New Year. But Eric Cantona, back in October after his ban of the previous season, galvanises the team, scoring priceless goals.

United climb closer to Newcastle, overtake them as Keegan's team falters and are crowned champions for the third time in four years when they win 3-0 on the last day of the season at Middlesbrough.

Best win 5-0 at home over Nottingham Forest in April; worst defeat 4-1 at Tottenham in January. Top scorer: Eric Cantona (14).

THE MANAGERS: Alex Ferguson 1986-

Best (1963-73), Brian Kidd (1966-74), Bryan Robson (1981-94).

GREAT MANAGERS: Ernest Magnall (1900-12), Herbert Bamlett (1927-31), Matt Busby (1945-69), Tommy Docherty (1972-77), Ron Atkinson (1981-86), Alex Ferguson (1986-).

HONOURS: 1907-08 – First Division champions,
1909 – FA Cup winners,
1910-11 First Division champions,
1935-36 – Second Division champions,
1948 – FA Cup winners,
1951-52 – First Division champions,
1955-56 – First Division champions,
1956-57 – First Division champions,
1963 – FA Cup winners,
1964-65 – First Division champions,
1966-67 – First Division champions,
1967-68 – European Cup winners,
1974-75 – Second Division champions,
1977 – FA Cup winners,
1983 – FA Cup winners,
1985 – FA Cup winners,
1990 – FA Cup winners,
1991 – European Cup Winners' Cup winners,
1992 – League Cup winners,
1992-93 – FA Premier League champions,
1993-94 – Premiership champions, FA Cup winners,
1995-96 – Premiership champions, FA Cup winners.

MIDDLESBROUGH
– The Premiership History

1992-93

PRE-SEASON: One of the founder members of the Premier League, Middlesbrough, managed by Lennie Lawrence, earn their place as runners-up to Ipswich Town in the old Second Division.

THE SEASON: The rush of adrenalin from the successes of the previous season carries Middlesbrough over an opening-day blip – a 2-1 defeat at Coventry.

What follows is a home and away double over Manchester City and a 4-1 routing of Leeds.

While home form holds good – only two defeats up to Christmas – away form turns from mediocre to bad.

In February and March four successive home defeats and five away send Middlesbrough plummeting down the table.

They finish with a draw and a win but it is all too late to stave off relegation.

Best win 4-1 v Leeds in August; worst defeat 5-1 by Aston Villa. Top scorer: Paul Wilkinson (14).

1993-94

PRE-SEASON: Left to lick their wounds following relegation, Middlesbrough stay quiet on the transfer front although Alan Kernaghan is sold to Manchester City at the start of the season for £1.5 million.

THE SEASON: The joy of three away wins in succession is diluted by a home defeat at the hands of Stoke City – yet Middlesbrough play like a team who feel they have a divine right to Premiership status.

Middlesbrough facts and figures

CLUB ADDRESS: Cellnet Riverside Stadium, Middlesbrough, Cleveland.

TELEPHONE: 01642-227227

FAX: 01642-248450

CLUBCALL: 0891-424200

The club was formed in 1876, turning professional in 1899.

PREVIOUS GROUNDS: 1877 – Old Archery Ground, Linthorpe Road, 1903-95 Ayresome Park.

RECORD ATTENDANCE: 53,596 v Newcastle United – Div 1, December 1949.

BIGGEST WIN: 9-0 v Brighton & Hove Albion – Div 2, August 1958.

BIGGEST DEFEAT: 0-9 v Blackburn Rovers – Div 2, November 1954.

TOP LEAGUE SCORER IN SEASON: George Camsell (59), 1926-27.

HIGHEST AGGREGATE SCORER: George Camsell (325), 1925-39.

MOST CAPPED PLAYER: Wilf Mannion (26) for England.

STARS OF YESTERYEAR: George Camsell (1925-39), George Hardwick (1938-50), Wilf Mannion (1946-53), Brian Clough (1953-61), Alan Peacock (1954-64), Eddie Holliday (1957-61 & 1965), Mick McNeil (1958-63), John Hickton (1966-77), Gary Pallister (1984-89).

GREAT MANAGERS: John Robson (1899-1905), Tom McIntosh (1911-1919), Peter McWilliam (1927-34), Bob Dennison (1954-63), Stan Anderson (1966-73), Bruce Rioch (1986-90), Lennie Lawrence (1991-94), Bryan Robson (1994-).

HONOURS: 1926-27 – Second Division champions, 1928-29 – Second Division champions, 1973-74 – Second Division champions, 1994-95 – First Division champions.

Middlesbrough end up as early-season leaders but it is a case of too fast out of the blocks as a series of draws and defeats towards the end of the year see them drop off the pace.

A run of four home wins, including a 4-2 victory over Millwall in February, revive the club's promotion hopes but away form continues to be disappointing and Middlesbrough fail to reach even the play-off zone.

Best win 5-0 v Barnsley in April; worst defeat 4-0 away at Tranmere in April. Top scorer: Paul Wilkinson (16).

1994-95

PRE-SEASON: Bryan Robson, formerly of Manchester United and England, is the new Middlesbrough player-manager.

THE SEASON: Robson marks his new career with a 2-0 home win over Burnley and Middlesbrough win their first four matches.

Another four-match home winning sequence in October indicates Middlesbrough not only as pace-setters but also as stayers.

The battle for promotion is close, however, and with only one automatic place available because of the Premiership being scaled down, Middlesbrough are harried all the way to the winning post. They just head off Reading, on 79 points, by three points.

Best win 4-0 at home to Portsmouth in December; worst defeat 5-1 at Luton in October. Top scorer: John Hendrie (15).

1995-96

PRE-SEASON: A new stadium – the impressive Riverside – and money to spend on players marks Middlesbrough's return to the Premiership with success rather than survival, the immediate aim. Nicky Barmby is the first high-profile signing from Tottenham for £5.25 million but more are to follow.

THE SEASON: Back in the top flight after a two season absence, Bryan Robson's men make a solid start with an opening day 1-1 draw at Arsenal, followed by a 2-0 home win over Chelsea to celebrate the opening of their new Riverside Stadium.

Home form is good and the Boro defence solid as they reach mid-November before losing their first home match, 1-0 to Tottenham.

Away form is also solid until the turn of the year with defeats against title contenders Newcastle and Manchester United and defending champions Blackburn.

But the signing of the Brazilian Juninho for £4.75 million in October captures the public's imagination and is followed by the arrival of countryman Branco on a free transfer.

Boro's season, however, tails off early and the plunge down the table follows five successive home defeats and an almost as uninspiring away run. They have enough points in the bag from the early season to ensure their place in the top flight.

Best win 4-1 over Manchester City in December; worst defeat 5-0 at Chelsea. Top scorer: Nick Barmby (7).

THE MANAGERS: Lennie Lawrence 1991-94, Bryan Robson 1994-

Peter Beardsley

Faustino Asprilla

NEWCASTLE UNITED – The Premiership History

1992-93

PRE-SEASON: Kevin Keegan is fined £1,000 for comments he made about referees the previous season and is to buy Robert Lee from Charlton Athletic for £700,000 a few weeks into the season.

THE SEASON: It is hard to believe that this is the same Newcastle side which was in real danger of falling into what had been the Third Division a year earlier.

Newcastle reach October 24 before their first defeat and that is 1-0 at home to Grimsby – the only home defeat they suffer during the season.

They have, by that stage, bagged a maximum 33 points on their way to the First Division title with 96 points – eight more than second-placed West Ham and Portsmouth.

Best wins 7-1 v Leicester and 6-0 v Barnsley; worst defeat 0-3 at Tranmere. Top scorer: David Kelly (24).

1993-94

PRE-SEASON: There is a blow when Peter Beardsley suffers triple fracture of the cheekbone in Ronnie Whelan testimonial at Liverpool.

THE SEASON: Newcastle show their Premiership naivety when they are beaten 1-0 at home by Tottenham on the opening day and then lose 2-1 at Coventry.

But they are to prove themselves quick learners and an away draw at Manchester United shows they mean business. Home becomes a fortress and of their last eight matches they win seven and draw one.

A string of good away results at the turn of the year – including wins at

Newcastle United facts and figures

CLUB ADDRESS: St James' Park, Newcastle-upon-Tyne NE1 4ST.

TELEPHONE: 0191-232 8361

FAX NUMBER: 0191-201 8600

CLUBCALL: 0891-12 11 90

The club was formed in 1881 and turned professional in 1889.

PREVIOUS GROUNDS: 1881 – South Byker, 1886-1892 – Chillingham Road, Heaton.

The club was previously called Stanley in 1881 and Newcastle East End 1882-1892.

RECORD ATTENDANCE: 68,386 v Chelsea – Div 1, September 1930.

BIGGEST WIN: 13-0 v Newport County – Div 2, October 1946.

BIGGEST DEFEAT: 0-9 v Burton Wanderers – Div 2, April 1895.

TOP LEAGUE SCORER IN A SEASON: Hughie Gallacher (36), 1926-27.

HIGHEST AGGREGATE SCORER: Jackie Milburn (178), 1946-57.

MOST CAPPED PLAYER: Alf McMichael (40) for N. Ireland.

STARS OF YESTERYEAR: Hughie Gallacher (1925-30), Jackie Milburn (1946-57), Len Shackleton (1946-48), Joe Harvey (1946-52), Bobby Mitchell (1949-60), Vic Keeble (1952-57), Bryan 'Pop' Robson (1962-71), Malcolm Macdonald (1971-76), Tommy Craig (1974-78), Chris Waddle (1980-85), Paul Gascoigne (1983-88), Mirandinha (1987-90), Andy Cole (1993-95).

GREAT MANAGERS: Stan Seymour (1939-47, 1950-54 & 1956-58), Joe Harvey (1962-75), Arthur Cox (1980-84), Jim Smith (1988-91), Kevin Keegan (1992-).

HONOURS: 1904-05 – First Division champions,
1906-07 – First Division champions,
1908-09 – First Division champions,
1910 – FA Cup winners,
1924 – FA Cup winners,
1926-27 – First Division champions,
1932 – FA Cup winners,
1951 – FA Cup winners,
1952 – FA Cup winners,
1955 – FA Cup winners,
1964-65 – Second Division champions,
1968-69 – Inter Cities Fairs Cup winners,
1992-93 – First Division champions.

Aston Villa, Tottenham, Everton and Norwich – help to propel Newcastle to a more than satisfactory third place in the table, but a good way behind Manchester United and Blackburn.

Best win 7-1 v Swindon in March; worst defeat 4-2 at Wimbledon in February. Top scorer: Andy Cole (34).

1994-95

PRE-SEASON: Marc Hottiger, Swiss World Cup full-back, is signed for £600,000 from Sion and Keegan then adds Belgian Philippe Albert for £2.65 million from Anderlecht and Paul Kitson for £2.25 million from Derby. All home games are to be for season-ticket holders only.

THE SEASON: Newcastle do not lose at home until the third from last home game – beaten 2-1 by Leeds.

Early away form is sparkling too, with wins at Leicester, West Ham, Arsenal, Aston Villa and Crystal Palace making them the early season pacesetters.

After that victory over Palace in mid-October, Newcastle do not win away from home until the last day of February.

The title challenge, once so strong, fades. Their Uefa Cup experiences end in the second round, beaten by Atletico Bilbao.

They finish sixth in the table and manager Keegan promises that the club has learned a valuable lesson. His most daring move is to sell his star striker Andy Cole to Manchester United in January for a then record fee of £7 million.

Best win 5-1 v Southampton in August; worst defeat 0-3 at QPR in February. Top scorer: Peter Beardsley (12).

1995-96

PRE-SEASON: The lessons learned from the previous season, manager Kevin Keegan moves to underpin the strength of the team by signing goalkeeper Shaka Hislop from Reading for £1.57 million, Les Ferdinand from QPR for £6 million, Warren Barton from Wimbledon for £4 million and Frenchman David Ginola from Paris St Germain for £2.5 million.

THE SEASON: Newcastle start as they did the previous year – flying! Home form is to be sensational with 13 straight wins until they are beaten 1-0 by Manchester United in March, a real six-pointer.

Away form is also good although the occasional surprise defeat slows them – including a 1-0 defeat at Southampton in September followed by late-season reverses at West Ham and Blackburn.

Newcastle however start January on top of the table and favourites for the title, but with the arrival of the Colombian Faustino Asprilla for £6.7 million from Parma and David Batty for £3.75 million from Blackburn, both in February, comes a slump.

Three successive away defeats, at Arsenal, a 4-3 thriller with Liverpool, and a 2-1 defeat at Blackburn, allow Manchester United back into the hunt.

A draw with Nottingham Forest leaves Newcastle needing to beat Tottenham on the last day of the season and United to lose. In the end Newcastle return their only home draw of the season – 1-1 and have to take second spot.

Best win 6-1 at home to Wimbledon in October; worst defeats 2-0 at Manchester United and West Ham. Top scorer: Les Ferdinand (25).

THE MANAGERS: Kevin Keegan 1992-.

Bryan Roy

1992-93

PRE-SEASON: Forest go into the season in confident mood – they finished eighth in the last running of the old First Division and at the end of the campaign had banked £1.5 million, selling Des Walker to Sampdoria. A few weeks into the season and Teddy Sheringham is sold to Tottenham for £2.1 million.

THE SEASON: Forest make a good start with an opening-day 1-0 win over Liverpool at home – the goal turns out to be a parting gift from Sheringham.

The sale of the former Millwall striker is to be significant because in spite of sticking to Brian Clough's fine footballing principles, Forest are impotent in front of goal. From September onwards, the highest position they reach in the table is 19th and even that is short-lived, although Stuart Pearce is appointed England captain.

Brian Clough announces he is to retire at the end of the season and after the opening-day victory, Forest fail to record another win until October.

Relegated in bottom place, Forest score just 21 goals all season and draw 15 blanks.

Best win 4-1 v Leeds; worst defeat 5-3 at Oldham. Top scorer: Nigel Clough (10).

1993-94

PRE-SEASON: Gary Charles is sold to Derby and Roy Keane to Manchester United for £3.75 million. Coming in, following a protracted transfer negotiation, is Stan Collymore for

Nottingham Forest facts and figures

CLUB ADDRESS: City Ground, West Bridgford, Nottingham NG2 5FJ.

TELEPHONE: 01602-526000

FAX: 01602-566003

CLUBCALL: 0898 121174

The club was formed in 1865, turning professional in 1889.

PREVIOUS GROUNDS: Forest Racecourse (1865), The Meadows (1879), Trent Bridge Cricket Ground (1880), Parkside, Lenton (1882), Gregory, Lenton (1885), Town Ground (1890), City Ground (1898).

RECORD ATTENDANCE: 49,946 v Manchester United – Div 1, October 1967.

BIGGEST WIN: 14-0 v Clapton – FA Cup 1st round, January 1891.

BIGGEST DEFEAT: 1-9 v Blackburn Rovers – Div 2, April 1937.

TOP LEAGUE SCORER IN SEASON: Wally Ardron (36), 1950/51.

HIGHEST AGGREGATE SCORER: Grenville Morris (199), 1898-1913.

MOST CAPPED PLAYER: Stuart Pearce (71 at end of June 1996) for England.

STARS OF YESTERYEAR: Jack Burkitt (1948-61), Joe Baker (1965-68), John Robertson (1970-83), Tony Woodcock (1974-79), John McGovern (1974-82), Peter Withe (1977-79), Archie Gemmill (1977-79), Peter Shilton (1977-82), Trevor Francis (1978-82), Des Walker (1983-92).

GREAT MANAGERS: Harry Radford (1889-1897), Harry Haslam (1897-1909), Bob Masters (1912-25), Billy Walker (1939-60), John Carey (1963-68), Brian Clough (1975-93), Frank Clark (1993-).

HONOURS: 1898 – FA Cup winners, 1906-07 – Second Division champions, 1921-22 – Second Division champions, 1950-51– Division Three South champions, 1959 – FA Cup winners, 1977-78 – First Division champions, League Cup winners, 1978-79 – European Cup winners, League Cup winners, 1979-80 – European Cup winners, 1988-89 – League Cup winners, 1989-90 – League Cup winners.

£2.2 million from Southend. Frank Clark – manager at Orient but an ex-Forest player – is Clough's successor.

THE SEASON: Tipped for an immediate return to the Premiership, Forest make a slow start to the campaign with only two wins in their first nine matches and, significantly, a 2-0 defeat at Crystal Palace, the team relegated with them the previous season and perceived as their main rivals for promotion.

Collymore scores his first goals in a 4-3 defeat at Bolton in September and this signals the change in Forest's fortunes.

They sign Norwegian international Lars Bohinen in November and an unbeaten run until February lifts them to sixth in the table. Then a five-match winning streak in March hoists them to second. Forest win promotion, nine points ahead of third-placed Millwall but seven behind champions Crystal Palace.

Best wins 4-0 v Leicester, 5-3 v Grimsby Town; worst defeat 3-1 at home to Millwall. Top scorer: Stan Collymore (19).

1994-95

PRE-SEASON: Dutch international Bryan Roy is the major buy for £2.5 million from Italian side Foggia. Otherwise, Forest remain quiet on the transfer market.

THE SEASON: New signing Bryan Roy scores on his debut – the only goal of the match at Ipswich Town. Roy is to go on to score 13 during the season.

Forest continue to make progress and play 11 Premiership matches before suffering their first defeat.

At the start of November they are second in the table but then lose four and draw two of their next six matches. The period coincides with a barren patch in front of goal.

Forest, however, never drop below fifth in the table and end the season with a bang, winning nine and drawing two of their last 11 matches. They finish in third place.

Best win 7-1 v Sheffield Wednesday; worst defeat 0-3 v Blackburn Rovers at Ewood Park. Top scorer: Stan Collymore (22).

1995-96

PRE-SEASON: Stan Collymore is sold to Liverpool for £8.5 million – a British record, but Forest manager Frank Clark does not rush to reinvest the money.

THE SEASON: An opening day 4-3 win at Southampton is supported by some solid home form and a mean defence on their travels. Forest do not lose in the Premiership until November 18, but when they do it is spectacular.

Playing at Blackburn, Forest are annihilated 7-0 and it signals a collapse in away form. They do not win away again until March when Sheffield Wednesday are beaten 3-1.

Forest become England's flag bearers in Europe, reaching the quarter-finals of the Uefa Cup where they lose 2-1 in Germany against Bayern Munich then 5-1 at home.

Blackburn also deliver a crushing home defeat for Forest when they win 5-1 at the City Ground in mid-April but Forest still have a significant effect on the Championship battle when in successive matches they lose 5-0 to Manchester United but then draw 1-1 with Newcastle.

Best win 4-1 against Wimbledon in November; worst defeat 7-0 at Blackburn. Top scorers: Bryan Roy, Jason Lee, Ian Woan (8).

THE MANAGERS: Brian Clough 1975-93, Frank Clark 1993-

Des Walker

Chris Waddle

1992-93

PRE-SEASON: Manager Trevor Francis keeps faith with the team which finished in third place in Division One the year before.

THE SEASON: Their first Premier League game is a 1-1 draw at Goodison Park, the Owls' goal being a rare strike from Nigel Pearson. They fail to win a game until mid-September, when they beat Nottingham Forest 2-1 with goals from Paul Warhurst and Graham Hyde.

Mark Bright is signed from Crystal Palace in September. He cannot prevent their failing to win in seven games and dropping to 17th. Seven wins in a row at the turn of the year sees their position rise. Paul Warhurst begins to play up front and scores four goals in as many games.

After a patchy end to the season they finish in seventh, with 59 points. A high number of draws at Hillsborough prevents their rising further.

Best win 5-2 at home to Southampton in April; worst defeat a 3-0 drubbing at the hands of Manchester City in September. Top scorer: Mark Bright (11).

1993-94

PRE-SEASON: Des Walker (£2.7 million) and Andy Sinton (£2.75 million) signed from Sampdoria and QPR respectively.

THE SEASON: Wednesday start disastrously. Their first game is a 2-0 defeat at Liverpool and they do not win until their eighth game, at home to Southampton. Paul Warhurst is sold to Blackburn for £2.7 million.

Sheffield Wednesday facts and figures

CLUB ADDRESS: Hillsborough, Sheffield, S6 1SW.

TELEPHONE: 0114 221 2121

FAX: 0114 221 2122

CLUBCALL: 0891 121186

The club was formed in 1867 and turned professional in 1887, becoming Sheffield Wednesday in 1929.

PREVIOUS GROUNDS: Highfield, Myrtle Road, Sheaf House, Olive Grove and Owlerton (known as Hillsborough since 1912).

RECORD ATTENDANCE: 72,841 v Manchester City, FA Cup 5th rnd, February 1934.

BIGGEST WIN: 12-0 v Halliwell, FA Cup 1st rnd, January 1891.

BIGGEST DEFEAT: 0-10 v Aston Villa, Div 1, October 1912.

TOP LEAGUE SCORER IN A SEASON: Derek Dooley (46), 1951-52.

HIGHEST AGGREGATE SCORER: Andy Wilson (199), 1900-20.

MOST CAPPED PLAYER: Nigel Worthington (63) for N. Ireland.

STARS OF YESTERYEAR: Ernie Blenkinsop (1923-34, Alf Strange (1927-35), Derek Dooley (1947-52), Albert Quixall (1950-58), Jackie Sewell (1951-55), John Fantham (1956-69), Ron Springett (1958-67).

GREAT MANAGERS: Robert Brown (1920-33), Billy Walker (1933-37), Harry Catterick (1958-61), Howard Wilkinson (1983-88).

HONOURS: 1895-96 – FA Cup winners, 1899-1900 – Second Division champions, 1902-03 – First Division champions, 1903-04 – First Division champions, 1906-07 – FA Cup winners, 1925-26 – Second Division champions, 1928-29 – First Division champions, 1929-30 – First Division champions, 1934-35 – FA Cup winners, 1951-52 – Second Division champions, 1955-56 – Second Division champions, 1958-59 – Second Division champions, 1990-91 – League Cup winners.

At the end of October, they are 20th and looking likely candidates for relegation. They begin to climb the table, Mark Bright's eight goals in eight games taking them into sixth place in February.

They go five games without a win to halt their charge to the top, Bright losing his Midas touch. They finish the season with nine games without defeat to finish the season in seventh, with 64 points. Once again they have failed to win enough games at home.

Best wins 5-0 at home to West Ham and Ipswich; worst defeat a five-goal rout at Old Trafford. Top scorer: Mark Bright (19).

1994-95

PRE-SEASON: Francis sells Carlton Palmer to Leeds for £2.6 million and buys Peter Atherton and Ian Taylor to strengthen a squad still missing Chris Waddle through injury.

THE SEASON: Another bad start for the Owls as they win only one game out of their opening eight, Bright and Hirst scoring only one goal each. Hirst is sidelined by injury in October and Wednesday are short of a striker until the arrival of Guy Whittingham in December for £700,000.

Waddle returns and immediately improves the Owls' fortunes. Whittingham scores four goals in his opening two games, and ends the season with nine. They go eight games without defeat to rise to eighth in February but again their form deteriorates.

They end the season in 13th with 51 points, the promise of mid-season once again proving short-lived.

Best win 5-1 at home to Coventry; worst defeat 7-1 at home to Nottingham Forest. Top scorer: Mark Bright (11).

1995-96

PRE-SEASON: David Pleat is made Wednesday manager. He sells Chris Bart-Williams to Forest for £2.5 million and buys Marc Degryse and Mark Pembridge from Anderlecht and Derby for £1.5 million and £900,000 respectively.

THE SEASON: The season begins badly yet again, with a 1-0 defeat at Anfield, but Wednesday are encouraged by a 2-1 victory at home to the champions Blackburn. Dan Petrescu is sold to Chelsea for £2.3 million.

Their form is patchy, a 6-2 victory at home to Leeds coming only weeks after 1-0 defeats against Middlesbrough and West Ham. They spend £4 million on Darko Kovacevic and Dejan Stefanovic, the former scoring four times for the Owls, but they cannot save the decline of the club.

They lose three games in March, including a disastrous defeat against Bolton, to leave them in danger of relegation. They win only one game in April and fail to lift themselves out of trouble. A draw on the last day of the season at West Ham is enough to guarantee their safety.

Best win 6-2 at home to Leeds in December; worst defeat 5-2 by Everton. Top scorer: David Hirst (13).

THE MANAGERS: Trevor Francis 1991-95, David Pleat 1995-

Ken Monkou

Matthew Le Tissier

1992-93

PRE-SEASON: In a busy close-season, the Saints' manager Ian Branfoot sells Neil Ruddock to Tottenham, Barry Horne to Everton and Alan Shearer to Blackburn for a then British record fee of £3.2 million. He replaces them with Ken Monkou of Chelsea and Arsenal's Perry Groves. Kerry Dixon and David Speedie also arrive at The Dell.

THE SEASON: Southampton struggle to find their rhythm early on, scoring just 12 goals in the first three months of the season.

They appear certainties for relegation before a spring scoring spree guarantees their survival. The defence continues to leak goals, conceding 15 in the last four away matches. Southampton finish in 18th position with 50 points, one more than relegated Crystal Palace. They win just three away games.

Best win 3-0 against Norwich in February; worst defeat 5-2 at Sheffield Wednesday in April. Top scorer: Matthew Le Tissier (15).

1993-94

PRE-SEASON: Under-pressure manager Branfoot knows he must produce a winning side. He signs combative Tottenham midfielder Paul Allen for £550,000.

THE SEASON: Another desperate fight against the drop into Division One. The highest position Saints achieve all season is 17th. They survive on the final day with a nerve-tingling 3-3 draw at West Ham.

With Southampton lying next to bottom, Branfoot resigns in January. In comes former Saints player Alan Ball. He signs Jim Magilton from Oxford for £600,000.

Southampton facts and figures

CLUB ADDRESS: The Dell, Milton Road, Southampton SO9 4XX.

TELEPHONE: 01703 220505

FAX: 01703 330360

CLUBLINE: 0891 121178

The club was formed in 1885, turning professional in 1894. Previously called Southampton St Mary's.

PREVIOUS GROUNDS: Antelope Ground, County Cricket Ground.

RECORD ATTENDANCE: 31,044 v Manchester Utd, Div 1, October 1969.

BIGGEST WINS: 8-0 v Northampton, Div 3 South, December 1921 and 9-3 v Wolverhampton Wanderers, Div 2, September 1968.

BIGGEST DEFEATS: 0-8 v Tottenham Hotspur, Div 2, March 1936 and 0-8 v Everton, Div 1, November 1971.

TOP LEAGUE SCORER IN SEASON: Derek Reeves (39), 1959-60.

HIGHEST AGGREGATE SCORER: Mick Channon (185), 1966-77 and 1979-82.

MOST CAPPED PLAYER: Peter Shilton 49 (125) for England.

STARS OF YESTERYEAR: Alf Ramsey (1946-48), Terry Paine (1956-74), Martin Chivers (1962-67), Ron Davies (1966-72), Mick Channon (1966-77 and 1979-82), Bobby Stokes (1968-76), Peter Osgood (1974-77), Alan Ball (1976-80), Kevin Keegan (1980-82), Peter Shilton (1982-87), Tim Flowers (1986-93), Alan Shearer (1988-92).

GREAT MANAGERS: Jimmy McIntyre (1919-24), Ted Bates (1955-73), Lawrie McMenemy (1973-85).

HONOURS: 1921-22 – Third Division (South) champions, 1959-60 – Third Division champions, 1975-76 – FA Cup winners.

An amazing 5-4 victory at Norwich in April turns the tide for Southampton, ending a seven-match run without a win. Again they finish just a point clear of relegation, in 18th place with 43 points.

Best win a 5-1 thrashing of hapless Swindon in August; worst defeat 4-0 at home to Arsenal in March. Top scorer: Matthew Le Tissier (25).

1994-95

PRE-SEASON: Danish forward Ronnie Ekelund joins on loan from Barcelona while eccentric goalkeeper Bruce Grobbelaar moves on a free transfer from Liverpool.

THE SEASON: Ball promises a more attractive playing style than his predecessor and the Saints deliver. They spend most of the season in mid-table, in spite of an incredible spell of nine draws in ten matches around the turn of the year.

Ball breaks Saints' transfer record in January when he buys Chelsea striker Neil Shipperley for £1.2 million, equalling it in March for Gordon Watson from Sheffield Wednesday. The season's only blackspot is the arrest of Bruce Grobbelaar on match-rigging charges.

Southampton finish in a comfortable 10th position with 54 points, their highest placing for six years.

Best wins 3-1 against Coventry, Ipswich, Newcastle and Crystal Palace; worst defeat 5-1 at Newcastle in August. Top scorer: Matthew Le Tissier (19).

1995-96

PRE-SEASON: Alan Ball cannot resist the lure of his old pal Francis Lee at Manchester City. Dave Merrington is promoted to The Dell's hot seat.

THE SEASON: With the dip in form of their inspirational skipper Le Tissier, Saints re-assume the role of Premiership strugglers.

Merrington reacts to their lowly placing by bringing England international Barry Venison back from an unhappy spell with Galatasaray in Turkey for £850,000 in October.

Memorable wins over title-chasing Manchester Utd and struggling Bolton chart Southampton's escape route, which is completed by a 0-0 draw with Wimbledon on the final day.

Saints finish in 17th place with 38 points, the same as relegated Manchester City. They win just two games away from The Dell, Merrington loses the manager's job and is succeeded in the close season by Graeme Souness.

Best win 3-1 over Champions-elect Manchester Utd in April; worst defeat 4-1 by United at Old Trafford in November. Top scorer: Neil Shipperley (13).

Glenn Cockerill

THE MANAGERS: Ian Branfoot 1991-94, Alan Ball 1994-95, Dave Merrington 1995-96, Graeme Souness 1996-

Martin Scott

Paul Bracewell

1992-93

PRE-SEASON: Malcolm Crosby is given the manager's job on a permanent basis after steering Sunderland to the 1992 FA Cup Final. He signs Shaun Cunnington for £650,000 from Grimsby and former England captain Terry Butcher on a two-month trial.

THE SEASON: Sunderland's season turns out to be one long struggle against relegation to the Second Division. A dismal October sees them hammered 6-0 at West Ham and slip into the bottom four.

A 2-1 defeat at Watford proves to be Crosby's final game in charge as he is sacked on February 1. Terry Butcher takes over as Player/Manager but fails to make an impact.

Despite eight home defeats, Sunderland escape the drop with a 4-1 defeat of promotion-chasing Portsmouth. They finish the season in 21st position with 50 points, having lost 14 times away.

Best win 4-1 v Portsmouth in May; worst defeat 6-0 by West Ham at Upton Park. Top scorer Don Goodman (17).

1993-94

PRE-SEASON: Butcher strengthens his side, bringing in goalkeeper Alec Chamberlain, commanding central defender Andy Melville and goalscorer Phil Gray.

THE SEASON: A roller-coaster start sees the Roker men lose 5-0 on the opening day to Derby, then beat Charlton 4-0 a week later. But they slip to the bottom as October arrives.

Sunderland facts and figures

CLUB ADDRESS: Roker Park Ground, Sunderland SR6 9SW.

TELEPHONE: 0191 514 0332

FAX: 0191 514 5854

CLUBCALL: 0891 12 11 40

The club was formed in 1879, turning professional in 1886.

PREVIOUS GROUNDS: Blue House Field, Hendon; Groves Field, Ashbrooke; Horatio Street; Abbs Field, Fulwell; Newcastle Road.

RECORD ATTENDANCE: 75,118 v Derby Co – FA Cup 6th rnd replay, March 1933.

BIGGEST WIN: 11-1 v Fairfield – FA Cup 1st rnd, February 1895.

BIGGEST DEFEATS: 0-8 v Sheffield Wednesday – Div 1, December 1911, 0-8 v West Ham – Div 1, October 1968 and 0-8 v Watford – Div 1, September 1982.

TOP LEAGUE SCORER IN A SEASON: Dave Halliday (43), 1928-29.

HIGHEST AGGREGATE SCORER: Charlie Buchan, League, (209), 1911-25; Bob Gurney, Cup and League, (228), 1925-39.

MOST CAPPED PLAYER: Martin Harvey (34) for Northern Ireland.

STARS OF YESTERYEAR: Charlie Buchan (1911-25), Bob Gurney (1925-39), Raich Carter (1931-39), Len Shackleton (1947-57), Billy Bingham (1950-57), Charlie Hurley (1957-68), Jim Montgomery (1961-76), Dave Watson (1970-74).

GREAT MANAGERS: Tom Watson (1888-96), Alex Mackie (1899-1905), Bob Kyle (1905-28), Johnny Cochrane (1928-39), Bill Murray (1939-57), Alan Brown (1957-64 and 1968-72), Bob Stokoe (1972-76).

HONOURS: 1891-92, 1892-93, 1894-95, 1901-02, 1912-13, 1935-36 – First Division champions, 1936-37 – FA Cup winners, 1972-73 – FA Cup winners, 1975-76 – Second Division champions, 1987-88 – Third Division champions, 1995-96 – First Division champions.

The season is one long struggle to haul themselves up to mid-table security. Terry Butcher pays the price with his job in December. Former Huddersfield and Scunthorpe manager Mick Buxton moves in to the hot seat. Four wins on the trot in March put the play-offs in sight.

The inconsistency returns, however, and Sunderland finish 12th with 65 points.

Best win 4-0 v Charlton in August; worst defeat 5-0 v Derby seven days before. Top scorer Phil Gray (17).

1994-95

PRE-SEASON: Polish international Dariusz Kubicki is Mick Buxton's only summer signing.

THE SEASON: A 2-0 win at Reading in October puts Sunderland in eighth position temporarily as they flatter to deceive. However, their anaemic attack manages just 19 goals in the last 28 matches.

Mick Buxton is sacked on March 29 as the Sunderland board make their fifth managerial change in three years. Peter Reid is appointed.

Another season of under-achievement on Wearside ends with another desperate fight to escape the drop. They finish 20th, just one place above the relegation places, having won just five games at Roker Park.

Best win 4-1 at Portsmouth in November; worst defeat 3-0 at Luton at Christmas. Top scorer Phil Gray (15).

1995-96

PRE-SEASON: Peter Reid makes his first signing in May when he persuades his former Everton and England team-mate Paul Bracewell to join Sunderland as player/assistant manager.

THE SEASON: A champion season for Sunderland as they end their five-year exile from the top division. A run of eleven unbeaten games provides the platform for their success before a thumping 6-0 victory over then leaders Millwall takes them top for the first time on December 9.

Sunderland's defence proves itself the meanest in the Division as they concede just 33 League goals.

Derby's draw with Birmingham guarantees Sunderland's promotion but they clinch the Championship themselves with a 0-0 draw in front of 22,027 Rokerites. They finish with 83 points.

Best win a 6-0 hammering of Millwall; worst defeats 3-0, at Ipswich and Wolves. Top scorer: Craig Russell (14).

Phil Gray in Northern Ireland strip

THE MANAGERS: Malcolm Crosby 1992-93, Terry Butcher 1993, Mick Buxton 1993-95, Peter Reid 1995-

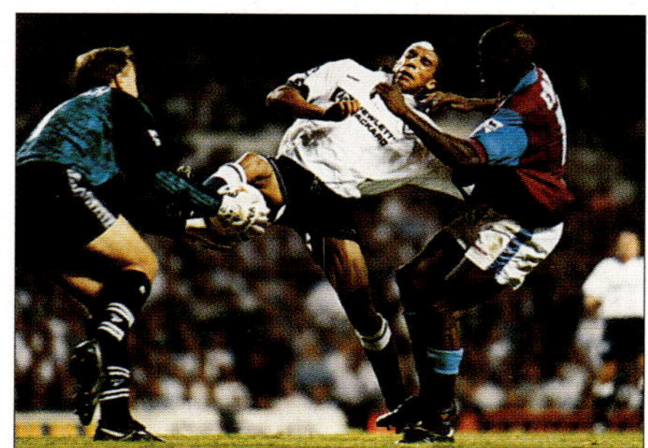

Chris Armstrong

Gary Mabbutt

1992-93

PRE-SEASON: Tottenham spend £2.1 million and end Teddy Sheringham's stay with Nottingham Forest – and reap the rewards. Sheringham scored 21 goals to become the Premier League's first top scorer.

THE SEASON: Tottenham's first Premier League game at Southampton ends in a 0-0 draw and they do not score a goal until the third match – a 2-2 home draw with Crystal Palace, Gordon Durie scoring their first goal.

In December Durie is cleared by FA appeal of feigning injury while playing against Coventry at the start of the season.

Tottenham finish their first season of Premier League football in eighth place in the table. They have 59 points from 42 matches – made up of 16 wins and 11 draws. Season ends in turmoil with Tottenham chairman Alan Sugar firing Terry Venables, the club's chief executive.

Best wins 5-2 v Oldham in December and 5-1 v Norwich in April; worst defeat 6-0 hammering at Sheffield United in March. Top scorer: Teddy Sheringham (21).

1993-94

PRE-SEASON: Steve Perryman resigns as Watford manager to become No 2 to new manager Ossie Ardiles. Neil Ruddock leaves for £2.5 million to join Liverpool. Venables starts High Court action for £1 million claiming "wrongful dismissal".

Jason Dozzell signs from Ipswich for £1.75 million.

Tottenham Hotspur facts and figures

CLUB ADDRESS: White Hart Lane, 748 High Road, Tottenham, London N17 0AP.

TELEPHONE: 0181-365 5000

FAX: 0181-365 5005

CLUBCALL: 0891-100 500

The club was previously called Hotspur Football Club between 1882-85.

PREVIOUS GROUNDS: Tottenham Marshes and Northumberland Park.

RECORD ATTENDANCE: 75,038 v Sunderland – FA Cup 6th round, March 1938.

BIGGEST WIN: 13-2 v Crewe – FA Cup 4th round replay, February 1960.

BIGGEST DEFEAT: 0-7 v Liverpool – Div 1, Sept 1978.

TOP LEAGUE SCORER IN A SEASON: Jimmy Greaves (37), 1962-63.

HIGHEST AGGREGATE SCORER: Jimmy Greaves (220), 1961-70.

MOST CAPPED PLAYER: Pat Jennings (74) for Northern Ireland.

STARS OF YESTERYEAR: Vivian Woodward (1901-09), Jimmy Dimmock (1918-31), Bill Nicholson (1936-54), Ted Ditchburn (1939-59), Len Duquemin (1946-59), Alf Ramsey (1949-55), Danny Blanchflower (1954-64), Dave Mackay (1958-68), Jimmy Greaves (1961-69), Alan Mullery (1964-72), Pat Jennings (1964-77), Glenn Hoddle (1975-87), Ossie Ardiles (1978-88), Chris Waddle (1985-89), Paul Gascoigne (1988-92), Gary Lineker (1989-92).

GREAT MANAGERS: Arthur Rowe (1949-55), Bill Nicholson (1958-74), Keith Burkinshaw (1976-84).

HONOURS: 1900-01 – FA Cup winners,
1919-20 – Second Division champions,
1920-21 – FA Cup winners,
1949-50 – Second Division champions,
1950-51 – First Division champions,
1960-61 – First Division champions, FA Cup winners,
1961-62 – FA Cup winners,
1962-63 – European Cup-Winners' Cup winners,
1966-67 – FA Cup winners,
1970-71 – League Cup winners,
1971-72 – Uefa Cup winners,
1972-73 – League Cup winners,
1980-81 – FA Cup winners,
1981-82 – FA Cup winners,
1983-84 – Uefa Cup winners,
1990-91 – FA Cup winners.

THE SEASON: Tottenham are to finish the season in 15th place – a position down to awful home form. Only four matches are won at White Hart Lane, the best a 5-0 victory over Oldham and only better results away from home saved the club from a worse fate.

The highlight of the season was a 2-1 win at Liverpool on August 25, 1994, but at home Tottenham went from October 3 until April 23 without a Premiership win – a run of 14 matches.

Best win 5-0 v Oldham; worst defeat 4-1 by West Ham at White Hart Lane. Top scorer: Teddy Sheringham (14).

1994-95

PRE-SEASON: Jurgen Klinsmann is the big signing for £2 million following the arrival of Romanian Ilie Dumitrescu, bought from Steaua Bucharest for £2.6 million. Yet the club faces starting the season minus 12 points and out of the FA Cup following alleged financial irregularities. Both those punishments were rescinded following appeals though the club are left with a £1.5 million fine.

THE SEASON: A good start is followed by three successive home defeats and in November Ardiles is sacked, No 2 Steve Perryman becoming caretaker manager. Gerry Francis is appointed new manager in late November. His arrival leads to a tightening-up of the Tottenham defence and a string of good results.

The Sheringham-Klinsmann partnership produces 38 Premiership goals, Klinsmann scoring 20 of them. The German, expected to stay for two seasons, announced he was leaving to play for Bayern Munich at the end of the season.

Tottenham finished seventh with 16 wins and 14 draws. Home form greatly improved on the previous seasons with ten wins compared to four.

Best win 4-0 at Coventry in December; worst defeat 5-2 at Manchester City in October. Top scorer: Jurgen Klinsmann (20).

1995-96

PRE-SEASON: Jurgen Klinsmann leaves for Germany and Spurs spend £4.5 million replacing him with Chris Armstrong from Crystal Palace, money more than recouped by the sale of Nick Barmby to Middlesbrough at £5.25 million.

THE SEASON: Spurs make a sluggish start, losing at home to Aston Villa and Liverpool and drawing at Manchester City and West Ham. But the picture improves with a 2-1 home win over Leeds and a 3-1 victory at Sheffield Wednesday. Gradually Spurs start to build up a head of steam.

The Sheringham-Armstrong partnership starts to gel and is helped considerably by the £4.2 million signing of Ruel Fox, from Newcastle, in October.

Spurs climb deep into the top half of the table but inconsistency at home stops them making any further progress as valuable points are dropped. They lose just four times on their travels and five at home.

The highlight of the season is a 4-1 New Year's Day win over Manchester United, Armstrong scoring twice. Tottenham's FA Cup ends in the fifth round when they lose 2-1 to Nottingham Forest on penalties following a 2-2 draw.

Tottenham travel to Newcastle for the last game of the season where a win would give them a chance of qualifying for Europe but in spite of taking the lead, they draw 1-1.

Best win 4-1 at home to Manchester United; worst defeat 3-1 at home to Liverpool. Top scorer: Teddy Sheringham (16).

THE MANAGERS: Peter Shreeves 1991-92, Terry Venables 1992-93, Ossie Ardiles 1993-94, Gerry Francis 1994-

JURGEN KLINSMANN: A World Cup winner in 1990 with Germany, he terrorised Premiership defences averaging a goal every other game. Born 30-7-64.

GARY MABBUTT: Signed for Spurs for £105,000 in August 1982. He has won the FA and Uefa Cups with Tottenham. England international. Bristol-born. Born 23-8-61.

TEDDY SHERINGHAM: Joined Nottingham Forest from Millwall in 1991 then went to Spurs for £2.1 million 13 months later. England international. Born 2-4-66.

CHRIS ARMSTRONG: A £4.5 million buy from Crystal Palace in June 1995 to replace Klinsmann. A proven striker, he also had spells at Wrexham and Millwall. England B international. Born 19-6-71.

DARREN ANDERTON: Signed from Portsmouth for £1.7 million in June 1992 after one full season in professional football. He has won full England caps. Born 3-3-72.

RUEL FOX: Signed from Newcastle in October 1995 for £4.2 million. Started his career with Norwich then went to Newcastle for £2.25 million in 1994. He has won England 'B' international honours. Born 14-1-68.

IAN WALKER: England Under-21 goalkeeper. Signed a five-year contract with Spurs at the start of 1995. Born 31-10-71.

SOL CAMPBELL: Midfielder capped for England at full international level. Started with the club as associated schoolboy, joining from FA School of Excellence. Born 19-9-74.

RONNY ROSENTHAL: Israeli international striker signed from Liverpool for £250,000 in January 1994. Began his career at Maccabi Tel Aviv. Born 11-10-63.

ERIK THORSTVEDT: Norwegian international joined Spurs from IFK Gothenburg for £400,000 in December 1988. Born 26-10-62.

Julian Dicks

WEST HAM UNITED
– The Premiership History

1992-93

PRE-SEASON: Having been relegated in the last year of the old First Division, West Ham sell Stuart Slater to Celtic for £1.5 million.

THE SEASON: An away win at Barnsley to begin the campaign is followed by two successive defeats as West Ham's hopes for an immediate return to the top flight look less than brilliant.

A 2-1 win at home to Watford relaunches the Hammers, who then win 3-1 at Peterborough and 5-1 at Bristol City.

A 15-match unbeaten run that starts in December puts them on course for promotion and then a final flourish – victory in their last four games of the season – proves just enough in a tense and tight battle.

West Ham finish on 88 points – eight behind champions Newcastle but level with Portsmouth. The Hammers pip Portsmouth by one goal for second place.

Best win 6-0 v Sunderland in October; worst defeat 5-2 v Tranmere in December. Top scorer: Trevor Morley (20).

1993-94

PRE-SEASON: Dale Gordon is signed from Glasgow Rangers for £750,000 and is the only major buy as the Hammers prepare for their first season in the Premier League.

THE SEASON: Not an auspicious start as Wimbledon win 2-0 at Upton Park on the opening day and then West Ham lose at Leeds United.

Victory over Sheffield Wednesday brings a brief respite but then seven goals are conceded and none scored in a home match against QPR and a trip to Old Trafford.

West Ham United facts and figures

CLUB ADDRESS: Boleyn Ground, Green Street, Upton Park, London E13 9AZ.

TELEPHONE: 0181-548 2748

FAX: 0181 548 2758

CLUBCALL: 0891 121165

The club was formed in 1895, turning professional in 1900.

PREVIOUS GROUNDS: Memorial Recreation Ground, Canning Town (1895-1904).

RECORD ATTENDANCE: 42,322 v Tottenham – Div 1, October 1970.

BIGGEST WIN: 10-0 v Bury – League Cup 2nd rnd, 2nd leg, October 1984.

BIGGEST DEFEAT: 8-2 v Blackburn Rovers – Div 1, December 1963.

TOP LEAGUE SCORER IN A SEASON: Vic Watson (42), 1929-30.

HIGHEST AGGREGATE SCORER: Vic Watson (298), 1920-35.

MOST CAPPED PLAYER: Bobby Moore (108) for England.

STARS OF YESTERYEAR: Vic Watson (1920-35), Bobby Moore (1958-73), Geoff Hurst (1959-71), Martin Peters (1961-69), Johnny Byrne (1962-67), Trevor Brooking (1965-82), Billy Bonds (1967-86).

GREAT MANAGERS: Syd King (1902-32), Charlie Paynter (1932-50), Ted Fenton (1950-61), Ron Greenwood (1961-74), John Lyall (1974-89), Billy Bonds (1990-94), Harry Redknapp (1994-).

HONOURS: 1957-58 – Second Division champions,

1964 – FA Cup winners,

1964-65 – European Cup Winners' Cup winners,

1975 – FA Cup winners,

1980 – FA Cup winners.

West Ham in fact suffer poor home form all season and win just six games on their own patch. Away from home, they do better with seven victories including successive wins at Tottenham, Oldham and Arsenal.

That is enough to leave the club safe in 13th place in the table on 52 points.

Best win 4-1 at Tottenham in April; worst defeat 5-0 at Sheffield Wednesday in December. Top scorer: Trevor Morley (13).

1994-95

PRE-SEASON: After 27 years at West Ham – both as player and manager – Billy Bonds is asked to relinquish the managerial seat and is replaced by his assistant, Harry Redknapp, who had rejected a return to Bournemouth.

THE SEASON: The bad home form of the previous season is not such a problem as West Ham win nine games on their own ground, although the season begins with a 0-0 draw at Upton Park against Leeds.

Away form is the problem and defeats at Manchester City and Norwich follow the Leeds match.

This means that West Ham are rarely clear of the relegation dog-fight but just keep their noses ahead to avoid becoming embroiled in the worst of it.

Record signing Don Hutchison arrives from Liverpool and old favourite Tony Cottee is back from Everton to lead the attack as West Ham finish in 14th place with 50 points.

Best wins 3-0 v Manchester City, Wimbledon and Liverpool – all home games; worst defeat 3-0 at Manchester City. Top scorer: Tony Cottee (13).

1995-96

PRE-SEASON: Matthew Holmes moves to Blackburn with Robbie Slater and £600,000 moves in the other direction. Also new is Marco Boogers, from Sparta Rotterdam, for £1 million.

THE SEASON: West Ham struggle early on, losing their first two matches 2-1 at home to Leeds and then away to Manchester United.

It is not until late September that they score their first Premiership win of the season, beating Everton 2-1 at Upton Park. By that point the club have re-signed Iain Dowie, from Crystal Palace, and his fearlessness in front of goal is to be a big boost to the club.

Successive away wins at Wimbledon, Shefield Wednesday and Bolton in late October and early November give the Hammers some momentum.

A burst of transfer activity in the New Year sees West Ham sign Ilie Dumitrescu, from Tottenham, for £1.5 million following a haggle over work permits, Michael Hughes joins from Strasbourg for £200,000 and Slaven Bilic, from Karlsruhe for £1.65 million. Don Hutchison goes to Sheffield United for £1.2 million.

The New Year finds West Ham in better form and they finish their season with nine home wins and five away. The Hammers draw their final match of the season 1-1 at home to Sheffield Wednesday, and that leaves them an impressive 10th in the table.

Best win 3-0 at Bolton; worst defeat 4-1 at home to Aston Villa in November. Top scorers, Julian Dicks and Tony Cottee (10).

THE MANAGERS: Billy Bonds 1990-94, Harry Redknapp 1994 -

Dean Holdsworth

Andy Thorn

1992-93

PRE-SEASON: Wimbledon buy Brentford striker Dean Holdsworth for £750,000 nine days before the season starts. Holdsworth's goals ensure Wimbledon's survival.

THE SEASON: Wimbledon's first Premier League game is at Leeds where they lose 2-1. Their first point comes at Sheffield Utd in their fourth game, but the Dons stay bottom.

Terry Phelan is sold to Manchester City for a club record-equalling fee of £2.5 million. Ex-Crazy Gang member Vinnie Jones returns from Chelsea for £700,000 and appears in a video glorifying soccer's hard men. Sam Hammam calls him a "mosquito brain".

A 2-0 win at Coventry in January takes Wimbledon out of the bottom three at last and sets them on their way to a final position of eleventh.

Best win 4-0 v Crystal Palace; worst defeat 2-6 by Oldham at Boundary Park. Top scorer: Dean Holdsworth (19).

1993-94

PRE-SEASON: Wimbledon sets their sights on Europe, Alan Kimble comes in from Cambridge, Gary Blissett from Brentford.

THE SEASON: The Dons have their best-ever season in League football. They finish sixth, a position which, a year later, would have qualified them for Europe.

They reach the quarter-finals of the Coca-Cola Cup and the fifth round of the FA Cup where they lose 3-0 to eventual winners Manchester United.

Wimbledon pick up 17 points out of 21 in April. Their 3-2 defeat at Goodison on the final Saturday keeps Everton in the top flight.

Best win 4-1 v Blackburn; worst defeats 4-0 at Leeds and Newcastle. Top scorer: Dean Holdsworth (17).

Wimbledon facts and figures

CLUB ADDRESS: Selhurst Park, South Norwood, London SE25 6PY.

TELEPHONE: 0181-771 2233

FAX: 0181-768 0640

DONS CALL: 0891-12 11 75

The club was formed in 1889, turning professional in 1964.

PREVIOUS GROUND: Plough Lane.

RECORD ATTENDANCE: 30,115 v Manchester United – FA Premier League, May 1993.

BIGGEST WIN: 6-0 v Newport County – Div 3, Sept 1983.

BIGGEST DEFEAT: 0-8 v Everton – League Cup 2nd rnd, August 1978.

TOP LEAGUE SCORER IN A SEASON: Alan Cork (29), 1983-84.

HIGHEST AGGREGATE SCORER: Alan Cork (145), 1977-92.

MOST CAPPED PLAYER: Terry Phelan (8) for the Republic of Ireland.

STARS OF YESTERYEAR: Dickie Guy (1968-78), Alan Cork (1977-92), Dave Beasant (1979-88), Dennis Wise (1984-90), Lawrie Sanchez (1984-94), John Fashanu (1986-94), Keith Curle (1988-91).

GREAT MANAGERS: Dave Bassett (1981-87), Bobby Gould (1987-90).

HONOURS: 1962-63 – Amateur Cup winners, 1982-83 – Fourth Division champions, 1987-88 – FA Cup winners.

1994-95

PRE-SEASON: John Fashanu leaves Wimbledon for Aston Villa in a £1.35 million deal. In nine seasons with the club, the striker hit 107 goals in 276 matches. Veteran forward Mick Harford signs from Coventry for £75,000.

THE SEASON: Wimbledon's season starts poorly. They win just two of their first 11 games, John Scales is sold to Liverpool for a club record £3.5 million and goalkeeper Hans Segers is implicated in the Grobbelaar alleged bribes case.

Joe Kinnear confirms his reputation for unearthing lower division players by signing defender Alan Reeves from Rochdale for £300,000. Striker Efan Ekoku arrives from Norwich for £1 million, and a seven-figure fee is paid to Millwall for Kenny Cunningham and Jon Goodman.

An up-and-down season for the team. They finish in the top half again, but with a negative goal difference.

Best wins 2-0 successes over Coventry, Crystal Palace and Manchester City; worst defeat 7-1 hammering at Aston Villa. Top scorer: Efan Ekoku (9).

1995-96

PRE-SEASON: The Wimbledon tradition as a selling, rather than a buying, club continues as Warren Barton moves to Newcastle for £4 million in June. Goalkeeper Paul Heald joins from Leyton Orient for £125,000.

THE SEASON: Six goals and six points from the first two games, Wimbledon's famed tenacity is still undiminished and they beat Liverpool 1-0 in their third home match of the season.

But then comes a slump, both home and away, which makes the pundits' claim that this time Wimbledon are going to be relegated, look about right.

Six consecutive away matches are lost while they go eight games without a home victory. Whether home will be Selhurst Park, leased from Crystal Palace, for much longer is in doubt. A new agreement is to be signed and Wimbledon play with the idea of making a "new" home in Dublin.

On the Premiership front Wimbledon love a scrap and Christmas is the turning point as they win away at both Chelsea and Arsenal while at home they claim another London victim, this time QPR.

The second half of the season results in away wins at Everton and Middlesbrough and consecutive home wins, over Nottingham Forest and Manchester City, ensure the Dons of another season in the top flight.

Best win 3-0 at home to Manchester City in April and away at QPR in August; worst defeat 6-1 at Newcastle. Top scorer: Robbie Earle (11).

THE MANAGERS: Joe Kinnear 1991-

Vinnie Jones

– The Deadly Dozen to send defenders running for cover

By Aubrey Ganguly

From Denis Law to Gary Lineker, Geoff Hurst to Ian Rush. No-one is more revered by fans than a striker. A clearance off the line or a field-splitting pass may be invaluable contributions to the game, but nothing competes with football's ultimate glory – scoring a goal.

A consistent goalscorer is a treasure to behold to such an extent that the budget of even the most fiscally-minded club goes out the window when a class striker becomes available. Since the creation of the Premier League in 1992, the major clubs have spent over £75 million on forwards, an astonishing figure even before Alan Shearer had boosted it by £15 million on joining Newcastle. But cost becomes irrelevant if a new arrival brings success.

Blackburn spent over £8 million in teaming up Alan Shearer and Chris Sutton but the subsequent season saw the pairing score 56 goals and Blackburn crowned champions. That success ensured there were no complaints about the seven-figure price tag.

And even when the outlay is enormous, clubs can quickly reap a return on their investment. Season ticket sales, merchandise and even share prices can all benefit from the arrival of a new "hot" striker. Of course, the merry-go-round lasts only as long as the goals keep coming. The game is full of players whose much-heralded arrival is followed a season or two later by a quieter departure.

A reduced, or even free, transfer to a smaller club has been the fate of many a striker once thought to have the world at his feet. The real mark of a great forward is the ability to score goals week in, week out, not just for one season but over a number of years. Since the Premier League began, an elite number of players have done precisely that.

Some are poacher kings of the six-yard box, others are masters of the long shot. A few are play-makers as well as phenomenal finishers but the common denominator is goals and lots of them. Scored in arguably the most difficult league in the world.

These – in reverse order – are the dozen deadliest marksmen in the first four seasons since August 1992:

Since signing for Sheffield Wednesday in Sepember 1992, Bright has been the club's top scorer three times.

He first made a name for himself at Crystal Palace, where he formed a formidable partnership with Ian Wright. However, the move to Wednesday proved he could go on scoring in the top flight.

More of an all-rounder than an out and out goalscorer, Bright has nonetheless proved to be a remarkably consistent striker, as well as a player confident in his own ability.

In 1994, Sheffield Wednesday's then manager, Trevor Francis, dropped Bright from the team, intending to make David Hirst and Paul Warhurst his main strike force. A transfer to Everton was on the cards but Bright stood his ground.

"I'll still finish the season top scorer" he claimed. And so it proved to be, with Bright going on to score 23 goals – helping Wednesday to semi-final spots in both the FA and Coca-Cola Cups, as well as a respectable seventh place in the Premiership table.

Often overshadowed by his strike partners, Bright has proved he can score at all levels. In a career that has encompassed Leek Town, Port Vale and Leicester City, as well as Palace and Wednesday, the one consistent in his career has been goals.

Now in his mid-thirties, and not always a regular in the first team, he has still managed his fair share of goals, proving old habits die hard!

No.11 **Peter Beardsley** (51 goals)

"The only way I'd ever substitute Beardsley is if he had to be carried off. He can't be replaced. He's got everything."

This is Kevin Keegan's opinion of Peter Beardsley. And it's not difficult to see why he rates his captain so highly.

Still a candidate for the England squad, Beardsley plays with the enthusiasm of someone 10 years younger. His goals and his presence often provide Newcastle with a much-needed stability.

In a career that has seen him at clubs where titles have been won and lost, Beardsley has played for a number of the big clubs.

Signed by Manchester United at 21 from Vancouver Whitecaps, he played only one game before being released and returning to Canada. A spell at Newcastle followed before he signed for Liverpool. Two League Championships later and he was on the move again, this time to Mersey rivals Everton.

Goals came, whoever he played for, as Everton partner Gary Lineker recalls: "He's such an all-rounder. He's not just a wonderful playmaker who controls and passes the ball so well, he scores goals and works hard for the team."

Kevin Keegan couldn't believe his luck when he got the chance to bring Beardsley back to Tyneside: "I really couldn't believe it when I got a call saying I could sign him. I probably broke the speed limit getting down to Wetherby that day. Peter's the sort of player you build teams around."

Beardsley himself shows no signs of letting up. His role for club and country as a deep-lying auxiliary striker has provided him with a glut of goals and the arrival of Alan Shearer could provide the incentive to score many more.

Since returning to West Ham, Tony Cottee has carried on where he left off for the Hammers – scoring goals.

Now in his thirties, he began his career at Upton Park in 1983. Then just seventeen, he made his debut against London rivals Tottenham.

Cottee scored in the 3-0 win and went on to hit 118 goals in 256 appearances for the club, before his £2.2 million record move to Everton in 1988.

Things didn't go so smoothly at Goodison Park. Frequent spells out of the first team, and three different managers, didn't help Cottee but he still managed almost 100 goals for the club, finishing as top scorer in five out of his six seasons there.

However, he wasn't happy and when the chance came to return to West Ham he grabbed it. "I learned a lot at Everton," said Cottee, "but I was sick of being made a scapegoat for bad results and I wanted some security."

Now back at the club he supported as a child, Cottee continues to prove himself a dedicated goalscorer.

Holdsworth joined Wimbledon in August 1992. Previously a prolific scorer at Brentford, he proved almost immediately that he could do likewise in the top flight.

His first season saw him become Wimbledon's top scorer with 20 goals. It also marked the first of his increasingly bizarre bets with the club's chairman, Sam Hammam.

Hammam promised Holdsworth a bronze bust of the striker if he could hit 20 goals. After the goals came, Hammam duly coughed up and the bust now has pride of place in the Holdsworth living room.

The following season saw him finish top striker again. This time Hammam had to kiss his backside in front of the rest of the team!

"After buying the bust, Sam suggested another bet the following season," explains Holdsworth, "but I wanted something that would benefit the whole team and not just me, so I suggested he take us all to Quaglino's restaurant if I got the goals.

"He agreed and said if I failed I could kiss his backside. That's when I said he had to kiss mine if I succeeded".

The pair have continued to strike their odd bets, with Hammam vowing at their last recorded meeting that he would buy Holdsworth a camel if he got 20 goals!

Bizarre, but obviously effective, as Holdsworth has continued to put away the goals – to such an extent that speculation grew during the 1996 close season that Alex Ferguson wanted to take him to Old Trafford. It hasn't happened yet but rumours continue to surface that the United manager has first option if Holdsworth leaves Wimbledon.

What can one say about Manchester United's enfant terrible? Cantona has proved to be the most controversial player of his generation, yet also one of the finest.

Credited with almost single-handedly making United a title-winning side, there is no doubt that his contribution has been vital.

A superb reader of the game and a wonderful passer of the ball, Cantona came into his own in the 1995-96 season as a scorer of vital goals. From what seemed an unassailable lead, Newcastle were left gasping as Cantona's goals inexorably closed the gap in the title race.

"Eric is the outstanding player of the season." said manager Alex Ferguson. "He is the best footballer in the country and over the past few months has gone about proving that. In that time his form has been simply sensational.

"He has done so much for us and scored so many vital goals. His composure in the target area is quite incredible."

French legend Jean-Pierre Papin agrees: "He is one of the world's best players, a unique talent. He is so instinctive."

Cantona seems now to have got his infamous temper in check without losing the spark that makes him such a talent on the pitch. Insiders at Old Trafford say he plans to finish his playing career at the club, which is good news for Manchester United but perhaps not the rest of the Premiership.

No.7 **Robbie Fowler** (65 goals)

After only two full years in the Premiership, Robbie Fowler was already its seventh highest scorer and the Liverpool striker will surely improve on that position in future years.

Voted PFA Young Player of the Year two seasons in a row, he made his England debut at the tender age of 21 and looks likely to become a regular before the World Cup in 1998. He made his debut for Liverpool in September 1993, in a Coca-Cola Cup tie at Fulham. He got a goal in that match but really turned heads in the return leg when he scored five!

A born striker, Fowler has rarely been out of the Liverpool side since. "I always go on the pitch feeling I ought to score," he said. "I've had that feeling since I was a kid. I've tried different positions but there's something about rattling the ball into the net."

Frequently compared to the young Jimmy Greaves, Fowler has been at Liverpool since he was 15, and even then he stood out.

"You could see at the time what a talent Robbie had," says Kenny Dalglish, who signed the youngster. "He used to play in the five-a-side games between the backroom staff and I always made sure he was on my side."

Ian Rush also remembers the young Fowler: "He had a talent you can't teach. I remember coming in and playing a match with the kids before we started pre-season training a few years ago. I saw this lad who could score from anywhere. I asked our youth coach Steve Heighway who he was. It was Robbie.

"He was only 14 and wasn't a big lad but he stood out simply because of his ability to score whenever he got the ball."

Undoubtedly Southampton's star player, and one of the most gifted individuals in the Premiership, Matt Le Tissier has frequently been the club's top scorer.

Although the 1995-96 season was not one of his vintage years, Southampton still offered him an extension to his current contract which should see him finish his days at the club – it was just another sign of their faith in him.

Officially an attacking midfielder, Le Tissier has nonetheless proved one of the most consistent Premiership goalscorers and one of the most spectacular.

Perhaps his finest goal came in the game against Newcastle in October 1993. Back-heeling the ball over his own head and into the edge of the Newcastle penalty area, Le Tissier then proceeded to volley it past one defender, beat a second and half-volley the ball on its second bounce into the net.

He is now the highest paid player in Southampton's history and regularly referred to by the locals as Le God. "You are now entering God's country," proclaimed a local newspaper advert. "Follow Matthew and the Saints every day."

The only bugbear in Le Tissier's career is his failure to break into the England team on a regular basis, although he hopes it could yet happen.

No.5 **Andy Cole** (66 goals)

Andy Cole's £7 million transfer from Newcastle to Manchester United was one of football's biggest surprises.

Cole had already established himself as a favourite on Tyneside. In his final full season there, he hit 41 goals to beat a club record set by the legendary Hughie Gallacher 60 years earlier.

Furious Newcastle supporters bombarded Kevin Keegan with protests at the decision to sell him and for a while it looked like the manager had lost the support of his "Toon Army". However, when the purchase of Les Ferdinand pacified Tyneside, it was the turn of the Old Trafford fans to worry over a dismal start by Cole for United.

Ultimately, all was not lost. Cole adapted to the United style of play and slowly began to refine his game. No longer an out-and-out goalscorer, Cole became a team player. He learned to hold up the ball, Mark Hughes-style, and contribute to the United attack.

He slowly started to win over the fans with his contribution to the team and the goals began to come. Just after Christmas, United played title rivals Newcastle – the perfect stage for Cole to deliver a goal. He didn't waste the opportunity.

A first-time shot hit with total precision past the Newcastle 'keeper had the Old Trafford fans on their feet and reminded everyone that a player who scored 41 goals in a season doesn't become a bad player overnight.

In a team renowned for spreading the goals around, Cole finally appeared to be getting his share.

Teddy Sheringham moved to Tottenham from Nottingham Forest in August 1992. The £2.1 million transfer fee seemed money well spent as he became the club's top scorer in both of his first two seasons there.

Then-manager Terry Venables described Sheringham thus: "Teddy is genuinely two-footed, as good as anyone in the air, the best around at bringing others into the play, and he scores goals."

All are traits that have helped establish Sheringham not only as one of the Premiership's leading scorers, but also as an England regular in spite of fierce competition.

One of his strongest attributes is his ability to play both as an out-and-out striker or as an extra midfielder, distributing the ball out wide when necessary.

His versatility makes him an ideal striking partner and he has put in impressive performances alongside Les Ferdinand and Alan Shearer for England and at Spurs beside Jurgen Klinsmann and later, Chris Armstrong.

Never the fastest of forwards, he recognised the need to compensate for his lack of pace early in his career when at Millwall with Tony Cascarino and has never looked back. "I know I'm not quick. I never have been, so I have to think quick, and that's what I do."

When Brian Clough left Nottingham Forest following their relegation, he admitted to only one mistake: "I should never have sold Edward Sheringham."

No.3 **Ian Wright** (71 goals)

Ever since he scored a hat-trick on his league debut for Arsenal, Ian Wright has been a prolific scorer for the North London club.

George Graham paid Crystal Palace £2.5 million for Wright in September 1991 and he proved his worth in his first season, scoring 24 goals in 30 matches and winning the prestigious Golden Boot award.

Graham described him as "among the top half-dozen British strikers I have ever seen. He lights up the pitch and the dressing room with the electricity of his performances and his personality."

A latecomer to the game, Wright didn't turn professional until he was 21 but seems to have been making up for lost time ever since.

In 1995 he became the first player ever to score in every game through to a European final, when he scored in each round of the Cup Winners' Cup on Arsenal's run to the final. It answered allegations that he couldn't score at the highest level. Nonetheless, Wright's England form never seemed to match the dizzy heights of his Arsenal performances.

As far as the Highbury fans are concerned, he can do no wrong. Last season saw Wright involved in a much publicised dispute with his manager Bruce Rioch that led to Wright seeking a transfer. The Highbury faithful were outraged and promptly demanded Rioch's resignation.

Fortunately for all concerned, the differences were resolved. Rioch has since departed but Wright looks set to continue his goalscoring for the Gunners under new management.

"I'm not going to compare Les Ferdinand with Andy Cole – they are as different as chalk and cheese. But if Les can match the 24 goals he scored for QPR last season then it would give us a tremendous chance of winning something."

So said Kevin Keegan in June 1995, after the £6 million purchase of the London striker. Ferdinand certainly kept his part of the bargain – 28 goals, including 25 in the Premiership, showed he was continuing where he left off.

"I go into every game thinking I will score because the service at Newcastle is so good," says Ferdinand. "If I don't get the ball from David Ginola or Keith Gillespie, it's arriving from Peter Beardsley or Robert Lee. With that sort of help I know there are a lot more goals in me."

Good team mates certainly help, but Ferdinand's goal scoring prowess is due to more than just quality service. "He's a world-class striker," says England colleague Paul Ince, "and so powerful. He's always going to give defences a lot of trouble."

His contemporaries agree. In 1996, Ferdinand was voted PFA Player of the Year. So what's next for the Newcastle striker with Alan Shearer alongside?

"All strikers dream of scoring 40 goals in a season. Andy Cole hit 41 here and that is an awesome record," said Ferdinand. "But if I keep going at the present rate, then anything is possible and I would dearly love to beat that record."

Since joining Blackburn in 1992, Alan Shearer has established himself to be the finest striker in the Premiership.

He has finished every season as one of the competition's top two scorers, except his first, in which he played only until Christmas. Injury kept him out for the remainder of that season but he still finished fifth in the scoring tables.

His consistency has been as phenomenal as his skills. A former PFA Player of the Year, he has proved that year in, year out, he will score goals and many believe he has the potential to become one of England's finest-ever strikers.

"The nearest comparisons I can make to other English strikers are Jimmy Greaves and Gary Lineker – but potentially Alan is better," said Terry Venables in 1995.

"Intelligence is the key to greatness and that is what he has. It's the sort of intelligence I normally associate with Dutch players – this talent for working out how to take a defence apart, piece by piece."

One of the most impressive aspects of Shearer is the quality of his overall play. Obviously a phenomenal goalscorer, he is also a great team player, one of the attributes that weighed heavily with Newcastle on signing him for £15 million in August 1996.

"He is always available as a get-out route for defenders under pressure," said David Pleat, the Sheffield Wednesday manager. "He never hides in a game and is always aware of his fellow strikers. Plus he's an excellent crosser of the ball."

His fellow players are equally complimentary. Ian Rush called him the most complete striker in Britain, while Dennis Bergkamp said he was the best in Europe. So how long before he is recognised as the world's No 1?

Saturday October 3, 1992

Blackburn Rovers 7 Norwich City 1

Norwich arrived at Ewood Park as the season's pace-setters and with ten games already under their belt led the Premier League by two points from second-placed Blackburn Rovers.

The East Anglia side had won 4–2 on the opening day at Arsenal and come back from 2–0 down against Chelsea at Stamford Bridge to win 3–2.

Blackburn, back in the top flight for the first time since 1966, had made a good start and their only serious blip was a 3–2 home defeat by Everton. This match would sort out the men from the boys.

As it turned out Norwich were 1–0 down within ten minutes and dead and buried by half-time.

Their chief tormentor was Blackburn's Alan Shearer, scorer of only two goals, but the creator of mayhem in the Norwich defence with his running.

He set up Roy Wegerle for the first when outstripping Ian Butterworth and pulling the ball back for one of those "thank you very much" chances beloved of strikers.

Next Tim Sherwood headed home and then the Shearer–Wegerle double-act did it again. Rob Newman pulled one back for the visitors but that did not disturb Blackburn a jot.

A minute before half-time Shearer chipped Bryan Gunn from 25 yards out to make it 4–1. Shearer was then fouled in the 63rd minute and Gordon Cowans scored with a free kick.

The sixth goal was driven home by Stuart Ripley and Shearer notched his second and the team's seventh with almost 15 minutes to go. Blackburn had powered to the top of the table.

"Gunn didn't have a save to make," said Mike Walker, the Norwich manager later. "He was always picking the ball out of the net."

Blackburn: Mimms, Brown, Wright, Sherwood, Hendry, Moran (Marker), Cowans, Ripley (Wilcox), Atkins, Shearer, Wegerle.

Norwich: Gunn, Culverhouse, Bowen, Butterworth, Sutton, Sutch, Crook, Newman, Robins, Goss, Phillips (Power).

Scoring: 1-0 (Wegerle 8min), **2-0** (Sherwood 27min), **3-0** Wegerle (32min), **3-1** (Newman 39min), **4-1** (Shearer 43min), **5-1** (Cowans 63min), **6-1** (Ripley 70min), **7-1** (Shearer 76min).

Attendance: 16,312.

Marksmen Alan Shearer, *far left*, and Tim Sherwood helped to pluck the Canaries' feathers in a 7-1 trimming

Saturday May 8, 1993

Oldham 4
Southampton 3

Oldham: Gerrard, Halle, Pointon, Henry, Jobson, Fleming, Redmond, Ritchie (Marshall), Milligan, Olney, Bernard.

Southampton: Flowers, Kenna, Adams, Widdrington, Hall, Monkou, Cockerill, Maddison, Le Tissier, Dowie, Banger (Benali).

Scoring: 1-0 (Pointon 29min),
1-1 (Le Tissier 34min),
2-1 (Olney 44min),
3-1 (Ritchie 55min),
4-1 (Halle 64min),
4-2 (Le Tissier 67min),
4-3 (Le Tissier 85min).

Attendance: 14,597.

Oldham had three matches left to play in a week – away to second-placed Aston Villa, home to Liverpool in eighth and then the easy one, home to Southampton in 16th place. The hard part was that they had to win all of them to ensure their place in the Premier League.

Oldham beat Aston Villa 1-0, conquered Liverpool 3-2 and then lined up against Southampton – not only having to win but also hoping that Crystal Palace, away to FA Cup finalists Arsenal, lost.

All went well for Oldham when Neil Pointon scored after 29 minutes but Matthew Le Tissier caused some flutters with an equaliser after 34 minutes.

Then in those crucial minutes before half-time, Ian Olney restored Oldham's lead and they traipsed into the dressing room to hear the good news that Palace were losing 1-0 at Arsenal.

After 19 minutes of the second half it seemed that Oldham had fulfilled their part of the survival plan as they led 4-1, further goals coming from Andy Ritchie and Gunnar Halle.

Matthew Le Tissier then led the fightback. He scored his second goal after 67 minutes and completed the hat-trick on 85 minutes, leaving Oldham to sweat through a nerve-jangling last five minutes.

Meanwhile at Highbury, Palace, having thrown all caution to the wind, were losing 3-0, conceding two goals in the last eight minutes. Oldham were safe.

"There's got to be a place in this business for the likes of us," said Oldham manager Joe Royle at the time. "There's got to be a bit of romance in a game that's predominantly run by money and power."

Oldham were relegated the following season – but ironically did the double over Southampton as they finally lost their place in the Premiership.

Twin pictures of Neil Ruddock, under siege after his dramatic late equaliser

Liverpool 3 Manchester United 3

A deep-seated rivalry and a battle between two great footballing dynasties, Liverpool's on the wane and Manchester United's in the ascendancy, was always going to provide a thriller – and so it came to pass.

At the time United, the defending Premier League champions, led the table by 13 points, although second-placed Blackburn did have two games in hand.

United arrived at Anfield brimming with confidence and for the first 24 minutes – precisely – played like a team from another planet. They were 3-0 up in that time.

First Eric Cantona's corner was headed home by skipper Steve Bruce after the Liverpool defence made a hash of clearing it. Next Ryan Giggs applied maximum pressure to Mark Wright, who had received a poor pass, and the Manchester United winger cheekily chipped Bruce Grobbelaar.

A few minutes later and Denis Irwin curled a 25-yard free kick into the net. Liverpool were incredibly 3-0 down and on their own turf.

Caution was thrown to the wind and within a minute of United's third, Nigel Clough scored with a low shot from outside the penalty area. Seven minutes before half-time, Clough had pulled it back to 3-2 with a similar goal only picking the other side of the net.

It was left to Neil Ruddock to save the day for Liverpool with a late equaliser. That Liverpool should concede three goals at home was remarkable, that they should then score three when apparently down and out was sensational – but to do it against Manchester United, miraculous.

"In a way, going 3-0 up was the worst thing that could have happened to us," said United manager Alex Ferguson. "It took the edge of us and they hit us with kamikaze tactics afterwards."

Liverpool: Grobbelaar, Jones, Wright, Ruddock, Dicks, McManaman (Bjornebye), Clough, Redknapp, Barnes, Rush, Fowler.

Manchester United: Schmeichel, Parker, Bruce, Pallister, Irwin, Kanchelskis, Keane, Ince, McClair, Cantona, Giggs.

Scoring: 0-1 (Bruce 9min), **0-2** (Giggs 20min), **0-3** (Irwin 24min), **1-3** (Clough 25min), **2-3** (Clough 38min), **3-3** (Ruddock 79min).

Attendance 42,795.

Everton manager Mike Walker celebrates survival with nine minutes to go to the season's end

Everton: Southall, Snodin, Ablett, Unsworth, Watson, Stuart, Horne, Ebbrell, Cottee, Rideout, Limpar.

Wimbledon: Segers, Barton, Scales, Blackwell, Elkins, Fear, Jones, Earle, Gayle, Clarke, Holdsworth.

Scoring: 0-1 (Holdsworth pen 4min),
0-2 (Ablett og 20min),
1-2 (Stuart pen 24min),
2-2 (Horne 67min),
3-2 (Stuart 81min).

Attendance: 31,297.

Everton 3 Wimbledon 2

Mighty Everton's place in the top echelons of English football hung by a thread – and after 20 minutes of the match against Wimbledon, a frayed thread at that.

It was once again a down-to-the-wire season with Everton below the survival line at third from bottom with one match to go – they needed a result and then wanted the teams above them to lose out.

The main target for Everton was Sheffield United, who on that final Saturday were at Stamford Bridge.

Everton had a disastrous start against Wimbledon, conceding a penalty after four minutes and Dean Holdsworth crashed home the kick. Another 16 minutes passed before Wimbledon added a second when Andy Clarke's shot was turned into his own goal by Gary Ablett.

A glimmer of hope was provided when Everton were awarded a penalty and Graham Stuart scored. And that was how it stood at half-time. Meanwhile in London, Chelsea were losing 1-0 to Sheffield United. Bad news for Everton on all fronts.

But just when it could have got worse, it got better. A furious Wimbledon raid on the Everton goal should have resulted in a penalty – at least that is what the Londoners claimed – and what is more, they said the video later proved that to be the case.

Instead Barry Horne pulled the match level with a counter-attack. Even so, would that be enough with Sheffield United 2-1 ahead in London?

Then, however, the season turned for the final time; the last twist after 41 matches and 80 minutes of the 42nd was settled by ten drama-packed minutes of football in London and Liverpool.

At Goodison Park Stuart scored with a long-range shot that bobbled past Hans Segers, the Wimbledon goalkeeper, and Everton had to hang on to their lead for nine more minutes. Meanwhile at Chelsea it was 2-2 only for Mark Stein to score in the last minute to make it 3-2 to the home club.

Everton preserved their 40-year status at the top of English football and Sheffield United were relegated.

Sheffield Wednesday 3
Tottenham Hotspur 4

Tottenham's Teddy Sheringham at the centre of celebrations after Jurgen Klinsmann's first Premiership goal

Sheffield Wednesday's Hillsborough had not been a happy hunting ground for Tottenham but they arrived on the opening day of the 1994-95 season ready and determined – not least to wipe out a six point deficit thay were starting with as punishment for financial irregularities.

But there was something extra from Tottenham for this game and indeed for the season – Hillsborough marked the first Premiership appearance of German World Cup winning striker Jurgen Klinsmann in a Spurs shirt.

The pre-conceived English perception of Klinsmann was summed up by the Sheffield Wednesday fan wearing a Klinsmann shirt, goggles and a snorkel. It was a notion that Klinsmann was to dispel with charm and humour off the pitch, and superb finishing on it.

Tottenham went ahead when Teddy Sheringham fired home the first from Darren Anderton's cross, then Anderton turned scorer when he poked home a shot following a flowing move which started with goalkeeper Ian Walker and took in Sheringham and Klinsmann.

Spurs led 2-0 at half-time but the Londoners have not been renowned in recent times for having the sturdiest of defences.

The second half was but 21 minutes old and Wednesday were level at 2-2. Dan Petrescu scored from a half-cleared corner and Colin Calderwood conceded an own goal as Wednesday's Mark Bright threatened.

Yet Spurs still had something in the tank. Nick Barmby took on the Wednesday defence and won, sliding a low shot past Kevin Pressman, then Klinsmann nodded home the fourth.

Wednesday, however, were still not done. Within a minute they pulled one back when David Hirst scored with a glorious volley and Tottenham were left to soak up the pressure over the last desperate seven minutes.

Sheffield Wednesday:
Pressman, Petrescu, Atherton, Walker, Nolan, Sheridan, Bart-Williams, Taylor, Sinton, Bright (Watson), Hirst.

Tottenham: Walker, Edinburgh, Calderwood, Barmby, Dumitrescu (Mabbutt), Anderton , Sheringham, Nethercott, Klinsmann, Kerslake, Campbell (Hazard).

Scoring: 0-1 (Sheringham 19min), **0-2** (Anderton 30min), **1-2** (Petrescu 54min), **2-2** (Calderwood og 66min), **2-3** (Barmby 71min), **2-4** (Klinsmann 82min), **3-4** (Hirst 83min).

Attendance: 34,051.

Stan Collymore is jubilant after blotting United's clean sheet stretching back over a remarkable nine-month period

Manchester United: Walsh, Bruce, Pallister, Ince, McClair, Cantona, Kanchelskis (Butt), Hughes, Giggs (Neville), Irwin, Keane.

Nottingham Forest: Crossley, Lyttle, Chettle, Pearce, Woan, Gemmill, Stone, Phillips, Roy (Bohinen), Collymore, Haaland.

Scoring: 0-1 (Collymore 35min), **0-2** (Pearce 62min), **1-2** (Cantona 68min).

Attendance 43,744.

Manchester United 1
Nottingham Forest 2

At the time this result was surprising enough but when put into context of the season, really remarkable.

Old Trafford was a fortress where visiting teams were not expected to score even a consolation goal, let alone win.

United had not let in a home goal since the Easter Monday of 1994 and here they were in December defending a run of nine matches – including games against some of the Premiership's leading clubs, having won the lot.

Three defeats away from home meant they trailed Blackburn Rovers in the table but United, as defending champions, were not giving up the fight.

The first shock came after 35 minutes when Stan Collymore, who had tormented the United back line, finally worked a way through when he thundered a shot past Gary Walsh from 25 yards after being fed by Brian Roy.

Though the United defence of Gary Pallister and Denis Irwin closed him down, there was nothing they could do to stop a goal being conceded at home for the first time in 1,135 minutes of football.

That became two when 17 minutes through the second half Stuart Pearce's shot took a deflection and flew past Walsh. Harsh luck for United, but given that Collymore had hit the post for Forest minutes earlier, perhaps it was divine justice.

Eric Cantona pulled one back and Forest went into siege defence for the angry last 20 minutes. Eight players were booked but the visitors held firm.

In fact, United conceded only four goals at home all season and Forest had collected two that afternoon – they were the only team to win at Old Trafford all season. A special match and a special victory.

Manchester United 9
Ipswich Town 0

Was it the slaughter of the innocents or the masters of excellence at their peak?

Alex Ferguson, the United manager, was sure it was the latter. "It was marvellous, the movement, the passing, the passion to play was terrific."

At this stage in the season United trailed Blackburn at the top of the Premiership by three points and had a goal average six worse.

By the end of the Ipswich match United had a goal difference advantage of plus two on Blackburn and though the Championship was not settled on that issue, it was still comforting for Ferguson.

And for Andy Cole, new to United colours at the start of the year, this was a grand day out as he scored five times – a Premiership record.

Roy Keane started the ball rolling after 16 minutes, shooting in off the post, then Ryan Giggs delivered a perfect cross for Cole to sweep home.

Mark Hughes hit the bar with a spectacular over-head shot but Cole was lurking again and hammered home the rebound. It was 3–0 at half-time and while United were clearly cruising there was no real hint of the massacre to come.

The period from the 53rd to 59th minute will, however, be the six minutes Ipswich fans would like torn from football's history book.

An Andrei Kanchelskis cross was helped over the line by Cole, Hughes crashed home a volley from an acute angle following Giggs' centre, then Hughes scored again – this time with his head, from another Giggs centre.

Cole, with the hat-trick in the bag, went on to score the seventh and ninth goals while Paul Ince hit the eighth with a chip from Hughes' lay-off at a free kick.

It's a Goal, Goal, Goal, Goal, COLE! Andy's five-shot is a Premiership record

Manchester United:
Schmeichel, Keane (Butt), Bruce (Sharpe), Pallister, Irwin, Kanchelskis, Ince, McClair, Giggs, Cole, Hughes.

Ipswich: Forrest, Yallop, Wark, Linighan, Thompson, Palmer, Williams, Sedgley, Slater, Mathie, Chapman (Marshall).

Scoring: 1-0 (Keane 16min), **2-0** (Cole 23min), **3-0** (Cole 37min), **4-0** (Cole 53min), **5-0** (Hughes 54min), **6-0** (Hughes 59min), **7-0** (Cole 65min), **8-0** (Ince 72min), **9-0** (Cole 88min).

Attendance: 43,804.

Newcastle 6 Wimbledon 1

Newcastle United: Hislop, Barton, Beresford, Peacock, Howey (Albert), Lee (Hottiger), Clark (Sellars), Ginola, Gillespie, Ferdinand, Beardsley.

Wimbledon: Heald, Cunningham, Jones, Fitzgerald, Earle, Holdsworth, Gayle, Harford, Perry (Goodman, Leonhardsen), Reeves, McAllister (Talboys).

Scoring: 1-0 (Howey 31min), **2-0** (Ferdinand 35min), **3-0** (Ferdinand 41min), **4-0** (Clark 59min), **4-1** (Gayle 60min), **5-1** (Ferdinand 63min), **6-1** (Albert 84min).

Attendance: 36,434.

The Kevin Keegan way is not just about winning at all costs – it is about winning with style, playing with panache.

And his Newcastle, having warned that they were a force to be reckoned with in the 1993-94 season and set the pace before falling off in 1994-95, were once again giving everyone a display of all that was best in skilful football.

Bolstered by some star buys, among them Les Ferdinand and David Ginola, Newcastle lined up against Wimbledon – a side few relish facing – with eight wins out of nine matches to their credit.

It was soon to be nine out of ten as Les Ferdinand, an England international but not in the side at the time, made a point to all about his abilities.

Wimbledon held firm for half an hour before Steve Howey set the ball rolling. His goal was followed by Ferdinand's first in a hat-trick when he headed home David Ginola's precise cross.

Ferdinand added another, then Wimbledon goalkeeper Paul Heald was sent off for a second bookable offence – leaving Vinnie Jones in goal. He made three class saves but there was no respite.

Lee Clark scored the fourth, Ferdinand completed his hat-trick and Philippe Albert made it six. Wimbledon's consolation came from Marcus Gayle.

Wimbledon had picked their side from a squad depleted by injuries and their manager Joe Kinnear acknowledged the size of the task afterwards. "The difference between coming here this season and last is about £20 million. That is the gulf between the two clubs," he said.

Indeed Wimbledon had lost only 2-1 on their previous visit and that was in the days before Newcastle's millions had brought the likes of Ferdinand and Ginola to the North-East.

Tottenham Hotspur 4
Manchester United 1

Tottenham had waited a long time for their first Premiership victory over Manchester United – but it was worth the wait as they pulled it off in considerable style.

Suffering with a number of injuries that meant they ran with a makeshift defence, Tottenham hit the post twice before they took the lead in the 35th minute.

Chris Armstrong played the ball to an unmarked Teddy Sheringham and from around the penalty spot he beat Peter Schmeichel with a low shot.

Tottenham's joy, however, was short-lived. Almost straight from the re-start Philip Neville broke down the left and Andy Cole touched home the centre.

Spurs scored their second in the crucial five minutes leading up to half-time. Armstrong's cross was headed on by Sheringham and Campbell finished off the job.

United came out for the second half with Kevin Pilkington in goal for Schmeichel, who had injured himself in the pre-match warm-up.

Minutes into the second half, Armstrong dived low to head in Darren Caskey's cross and then, left unmarked again, Armstrong scored Tottenham's fourth and his second when he powered home Sheringham's centre with a precisely-placed header.

It was United's worst Premiership defeat since they lost 4-1 to QPR on New Year's Day 1992. It also meant that Newcastle were leading the table by four points and with two games in hand on United.

Tottenham had displayed clinical finishing against a Manchester United side that scored one goal from 22 attempts in the match.

First footing. Teddy Sheringham celebrates his captaincy role with a priceless opening goal on New Year's Day

Tottenham: Walker, Austin, Calderwood, Nethercott, Edinburgh, Rosenthal, Campbell, Caskey, Dumitrescu (McMahon), Armstrong, Sheringham.

Manchester United: Schmeichel (Pilkington), Parker, G Neville, Prunier, P Neville (Sharpe), Beckham, Butt, Keane (McClair), Giggs, Cantona, Cole.

Scoring: 1-0 (Sheringham 35min), **1-1** (Cole 36min), **2-1** (Campbell 45min), **3-1** (Armstrong 48min), **4-1** (Armstrong 66min).

Attendance: 32,852.

Stan 'The Man' Collymore sinks Newcastle with a last-minute goal after 'a terrific game of football'

Liverpool: James, Wright (Harkness), Scales, Ruddock, McAteer, Redknapp, Jones (Rush), Barnes, McManaman, Fowler, Collymore.

Newcastle United: Srnicek, Beresford, Howey (Peacock), Albert, Watson, Batty, Lee, Beardsley, Ginola, Asprilla, Ferdinand.

Scoring: 1-0 (Fowler 2min), **1-1** (Ferdinand 10min), **1-2** (Ginola 14min), **2-2** (Fowler 55min), **2-3** (Asprilla 57min), **3-3** (Collymore 68min), **4-3** (Collymore 90min).

Attendance: 40,702.

Liverpool 4 Newcastle United 3

The biggest showdown yet in the Premiership title race for 1995-96, this clash did more than live up to expectations – it took English football to new heights of thrills, skills and excitement.

Remaining cool and aloof was impossible even for football fans with no particular bias towards either Liverpool or Newcastle.

The action started immediately. The clock had just clicked past a minute when Stan Collymore's cross was headed down and over the line by Robbie Fowler.

Newcastle remained calm, took control and after ten minutes were level when Faustino Asprilla fed Les Ferdinand and he cracked the ball home. Newcastle then went ahead.

David Ginola outran the Liverpool defence and fired home as Jason McAteer tried to close him down. That was the way it stayed until half-time and had the second half ended with the score at 2–1, the public would have still felt they had seen a match.

However, there was more to come. The second half was more thriling than the first as fortunes ebbed and flowed. Fowler arrived at full speed to hammer home a volley and make it 2–2 after just ten minutes.

Again Newcastle nosed in front with Asprilla picking up Robert Lee's pass and having the strength and guile to beat the Liverpool defence.

Both goalkeepers, Newcastle's Pavel Srnicek and David James of Liverpool, made telling saves before Liverpool levelled with Collymore poking home a shot for 3–3.

The home side then stole the show with the last move of the match. The old warriors Ian Rush, on as a substitute, and John Barnes were the instigators and Collymore finished it all off with a fiercely-angled drive.

"Win or lose the title, we won't play any differently otherwise I'll go," said Kevin Keegan, the Newcastle manager, at the end. "It was a classic, a terrific game of football and perhaps I don't feel as disappointed as I should do after sitting there watching it."

Sentiments that earned a universal chorus of "So say all of us."

Every English field has a foreign corner – at least that was the case with English football in 1996 as players in the Premiership hailed from Denmark, Holland or France almost as often as they came from Dagenham, Hull or Folkestone.

Ten years ago players from outside the British Isles received admiring glances and added a few spectators to the attendance but in the 1995-96 season more than 120 foreigners representing five continents and 37 different countries were registered with the Premier League or Football League.

The money that is flowing through the Premiership means that although Newcastle and Manchester United have the resources and the inclination to spend huge fees on players like Matthew Le Tissier, Darren Anderton, Steve Stone and Tony Adams, they are often unable to prise them away from their clubs.

Even smaller clubs like Southampton can satisfy the wage demands of star players like the much-coveted Le Tissier, thus preventing a move within the Premiership. Because of that, every country in the world has become a potential market-place.

West Ham's Harry Redknapp led the way in 1995-96 – at the club where the original Football Academy was born. Americans, Croatians, Romanians, Danes, Australians, and even a few Englishmen, battled for places in the Hammers' side of 1996.

Redknapp embodies the Alan Ball and Howard Wilkinson philosophy that above all else foreign players represent value for money.

"If I was suddenly handed £7 million – the price Manchester United paid for Andy Cole – then I would have to look abroad, simply because you get better value for money", says Redknapp.

"There are bargains out there and no-one can blame a manager for looking."

Redknapp is not immune from his own disasters, which have included Marco Boogers, but he has a tried and tested method for assessing his players from abroad.

"The only way you can establish who will cope is by getting them on a trial for a couple of weeks," he says.

"You need to see them out on Chadwell Heath on a cold, muddy day to find out if they fancy it."

The 1995-96 season will go down in history as the time when the foreigners really made their mark.

Ossie Ardiles and Ricky Villa paved the way after the 1978 World Cup, but it was in the 1995-96 season when the floodgates really opened, during a season when the Bosman ruling made movement between clubs in Europe far easier.

Newcastle was gripped with David Ginola and Faustino Asprilla fever and the new Riverside Stadium was full of sombreros and coffee beans to welcome Juninho and Branco, their Brazilian imports.

Manchester United have been mesmerised for seasons by the skill of Eric Cantona but now he has been joined by Dennis Bergkamp at Arsenal and Ruud Gullit at Chelsea.

David Ginola

Faustino Asprilla

Above: Dennis Bergkamp
Above right: Ossie Ardiles and Jurgen Klinsmann
Opposite: Jurgen again – still smiling in a pose so familiar to Spurs' fans

Jimmy Armfield, the technical adviser at the Football Association, has marvelled at the foreign legion of the 1996-97 season.

"The repercussions of the Bosman case need addressing but I'm not sure what the answer is yet. On one Saturday in 1995-96, there were only eight English goalkeepers playing in the Premiership," says Armfield.

"But I don't think we should even be talking of putting a brake on it. Some of the foreigners are setting a very good technical example. They are thrilling the spectators.

"I don't blame the clubs for going abroad because they're only doing what's best for themselves. But the fact that they're going abroad suggests that there's nothing for them to buy here and that's the greatest worry."

Terry Venables agrees, adding: "If you are a young striker and you can't learn from Jurgen Klinsmann, you're not paying attention."

Before the 1994 World Cup when the world-wide explosion really took hold in Britain, clubs were content to look to Scandinavia for new talent.

Restrictions on work permits pre-Bosman meant that it was easier for Manchester United to sign Peter Schmeichel and for Liverpool to snap up Torben Piechnik.

Brian Clough opened the floodgates from Scandinavia in 1981 when he signed Einar Aas for Nottingham Forest.

The proliferation of Scandinavians in England led to 10 of Norway's 22-man squad at the 1994 World Cup coming from the Premiership or Endsleigh League.

Former Scottish international David Hay managed Lillestrom before returning to England and the assistant manager's job at Swindon.

Hay brought Jan Aage Fjortoft back to Swindon and said: "The Scandinavian players do not offer anything revolutionary to the English game but what they do bring is dedication, ambition and a will to improve."

The status of the leagues in Scandinavia also contributed to the flood and Hay added: "The best players can just about make a living by staying at home but they also all move abroad to make a full-time career in the game.

"They tend to prove a bonus to English clubs in that they're often used to training harder and longer than their English counterparts despite playing only part-time in their own countries."

Cantona has been the most successful import with back-to-back

Championship medals with Leeds United and Manchester United but in the charisma stakes it was Klinsmann who won the plaudits.

Although always remembered for his mad moment at Selhurst Park, Cantona's mercurial talent ensured even that was put to the back of people's minds the following season when he was named Footballer of the Year.

His manager Alex Ferguson is unstinting in his praise for the Frenchman, who carried United, almost singlehandedly at times, through the 1995-96 season.

"Eric is the outstanding player of the season," said Ferguson.

"He is the best footballer in the country and in 1996 he has gone about proving that. In that time Eric's form has been simply sensational.

"Eric has done so much for us and scored so many vital goals. His composure in the target area is quite incredible."

Cantona's biggest obstacle in 1996 was to convert from sinner to saint after the Selhurst Park incident and he stunned most of football with his exemplary behaviour.

Former Footballer of the Year Frank McLintock said: "I never thought he'd be able to conduct himself so unbelievably well with his temperament.

"I was convinced other players were going to wind him up, get him at it, but it's almost as though he's made up his mind never to let Manchester United down again."

The impact of the foreign legion was perhaps best demonstrated by Cantona's rival for the Footballer of the Year, Dutchman Ruud Gullit, a year after the title was won by Klinsmann.

England's Robbie Fowler was third with United's captain Steve Bruce pushing for the award.

McLintock said before the result was announced: "I hate to talk down the possibility of Steve Bruce winning it because he might not get the chance again, but Cantona and Gullit reach the areas that ordinary players like us don't.

"They reach a different plane that is beyond us.

"They are way ahead of any other players in the country at the moment. Their technique is superb, they are physically strong and they've got the knack of being able to play without being full out.

"They seem to contain their energy and are never boiling over like some British players, who play flat out with fists clenched.

"I don't want to decry our players because I think we are terrific value for money in many ways. But Cantona and Gullit have an air of superiority about them - they are almost majestic."

Gullit was joined by another famous Dutchman in 1995, Dennis Bergkamp, who arrived at Arsenal from Inter Milan for £7.5 million.

"Every Dutch player who has gone to England seems to enjoy his football," said Bergkamp. "The quality of the game in England has improved immensely. It is not just kick-and-rush football, like it used to be.

"The Premiership is a huge success. The stadiums are full and money is no longer a problem. That's why players don't need to turn their backs on England any longer.

"There is an exodus of players from the Netherlands to England and I can understand why."

The Dutch duo are currently lighting up the Premiership but the ease at which they were accepted, despite the pain they inflicted on England supporters, was increased by the success of their compatriots Arnold Muhren and Frans Thijssen.

Muhren was a hero in Ipswich from the minute he moved to Portman Road in 1978, linking up later in his stay with Thijssen, and their performances in English football raised their profile in Holland as well.

Andrei Kanchelskis

Branco

Savo Milosevic
Opposite: Ruud Gullit

Their manager at Ipswich, Bobby Robson, recalls: "Arnold and Frans have had more publicity in Holland than they ever had while they were playing there."

Muhren missed just one match in his first season at Ipswich and was named the club's Player of the Year

When he was one of only a handful of foreign players in the English top flight, Muhren said: "Other players in Holland would like to come here because the football is better.

"It is too much like a game of chess over there, not so exciting for the spectators."

Even in those early days of the foreign invasion, overseas transfers represented great value for money.

Muhren cost just £140,000 and Robson says: "Signing Arnold was possibly the best bit of transfer business I ever did for Ipswich.

"I became so frustrated with trying to sign players in England where I was being quoted ridiculous prices, I decided to try Holland."

On Tyneside they have their own heroes – Ginola, Philippe Albert and Asprilla are more than a match for Cantona, Gullit, Juninho and Bergkamp in the eyes of those in black and white.

And Europe isn't the only breeding ground for great Premiership players of 1996 – Asprilla arrived from South America when Ghanian Tony Yeboah had already made his mark.

Yeboah's manager Howard Wilkinson was in no doubt over the impact he could make in England and a string of blockbuster goals at the start of the 1995-96 season backed up his faith.

Wilkinson said: "I don't see why Tony cannot have as much of an impact over here as Cantona. His pedigree is just as good as Eric's.

"Tony's physical strength is quite amazing. I bet that two-thirds of his body-weight is in his legs."

The arrival of stars like Gullit, Bergkamp, Cantona, Yeboah and Asprilla was made possible by a little Argentinian, Ossie Ardiles, who landed at White Hart Lane after the 1978 World Cup with his fellow South American midfielder Ricardo Villa.

Steve Perryman, who played with Ardiles and then was assistant manager

Above: Dan Petrescu
Above left: Tony Yeboah

under him when the Argentinian returned to Tottenham as manager, explained the lift the duo gave to the club and English football in general at the end of the Seventies.

Perryman said: "Suddenly we were on a different planet. We had some ordinary years but when those two arrived, everyone wanted to know us. We were a team with style again.

"There were a few good foreign players in my day. You learn from the goods ones. Look at Klinsmann."

Ardiles and Villa were certainly credited with leading the contemporary foreign invasion but Lawrie McMenemy bought Yugoslavian Ivan Golac for Southampton just days before the Argentinians arrived in England.

"When Tottenham signed Villa and Ardiles it totally overshadowed Golac but I knew what I'd got, a tremendously skilful, attacking style of full-back who lifted the whole club," says McMenemy.

"He brought something new to our game and was value for money. Klinsmann had a fantastic effect at Tottenham. When we played them towards the end of the season, before it was all doom and gloom, and then he arrived and it was hard to get a ticket to watch them.

"Lads like Darren Anderton and Nicky Barmby were inspired by him, they were physically lifted by his presence and worked hard themselves as a result."

McMenemy while welcoming the foreign players does temper his enthusiasm with some caution.

He adds: "When I signed Golac I also brought over a Yugoslavian goalkeeper, Ivan Katalinic, who, unlike Golac, couldn't speak English and couldn't adapt to our style of play.

"That was a warning to me that while some foreigners can adapt to the English way of life as well as our game, it doesn't always work.

"From an England point of view the only position that's really suffered from the influx of foreigners is that of goalkeeper. We're no longer getting that conveyor belt coming through."

Before Ardiles, any foreign players would stand out in a crowd – in the Fifties at Newcastle and Barnsley the amazing Robledo brothers, George and Ted, at Manchester City was Bert Trautmann, the prisoner-of-war turned first-

Above: Jan-Aage Fjortoft
Above right: Dmitri Kharine

team goalkeeper who played in the 1956 Cup Final with a broken neck, and who can forget Albert Johanneson, the South African at Leeds?

The foreign legion have their detractors and not only managers who have bought the flops but from the players' union, the Professional Footballers' Association.

Gordon Taylor, the PFA's Chief Executive, is concerned about the calibre of some of the arrivals and refused to support Marc Hottiger and Ilie Dumitrescu's applications to renew their work permits in the 1995-96 season.

Taylor said: "You don't want people coming in who are no better than the people here, simply cheaper.

"Not so long ago we were teaching the Americans how to play. Now we've got work permits for them piling up on my desk. It could be disastrous for us."

Speaking before Gullit's and Bergkamp's arrival, Taylor added: "Since Ossie Ardiles came here 16 years ago, the vast majority of foreign players – with no disrespect – haven't adapted.

"I think we should bear in mind what happened to English cricket. Not enough attention was given to our own talent."

Taylor's fears have been realised at several clubs where the foreign disasters have outnumbered their successes.

Everyone remembers the success of the Gullits and the Cantonas but history shows us that foreign transfers are a risky business with far more failures than successes.

Argentinian Alberto Tarantini, who arrived at Birmingham after the 1978 World Cup, was perhaps the most famous foreign flop. An ever-present in the World Cup he left St Andrews after a turbulent spell of 23 league games.

French international star Didier Six arrived at Villa Park in 1984 before making a quick return across the Channel.

Juninho has been a great success in the North-East, of course, but in 1987 another Brazilian, Mirandinha, travelled to Newcastle for a massive £575,000.

Signed on the basis of his performance against England at Wembley earlier that season, Mirandinha never looked the same player when faced with the cold English winter.

But as long as the English game is able to attract players of the calibre of Cantona, Gullit, Ginola and Juninho, in at least one corner of England there will be a foreign field.

The moment Lee Sharpe turned up outside Old Trafford his car was surrounded by a mass of jubilant fans, ready to celebrate, ready to party and ready to acclaim their heroes.

Sharpe was hoisted high on the shoulders of the swaying throng. It was that sort of night. The night Manchester United won the League championship.

United's wait had been long and arduous, having been forced to see their great rivals Liverpool win title after title, so when Sharpe arrived at the ground it was understandable that the fans should descend on him, one of the heroes, with a chorus of "We are the Champions".

Sharpe had a match the next day, against Blackburn, but no-one really cared that much as the game that counted had just taken place. United's nearest challengers, Aston Villa, had lost 1-0 at Oldham, to a Nick Henry goal.

Villa's defeat meant they could not catch the Red Devils. For many United fans who had endured 26 years without being able to call themselves the best in the country, it was hard to believe that the first Premier League title would rest in the Old Trafford trophy cabinet.

Lee Sharpe

Sharpe eventually managed to escape from Old Trafford and joined the other players for an impromptu party at captain Steve Bruce's house.

The whole squad had stories to tell about how they avoided the natural tension of watching or monitoring on the radio the Villa and Oldham match.

Alex Ferguson, the United manager, played golf, others stayed in the garden, not daring to think about what would happen if their Lancashire neighbours beat Villa. The form book presumed the title would rest on their two remaining games.

The game against Blackburn 24 hours after the confirmation that United were Champions turned into a giant party with just over 40,000 invitations and Alan Shearer et al just bit players as United won the game 3-1.

Even Gary Pallister, goalless all season, scored and that was direct from a free kick. Everyone connected with United was walking on air and the 1992-93 Premier League trophy was passed from hand to hand.

"It's like being the uninvited guest at a party," commented Kenny Dalglish, the Blackburn manager, who knew the minute the United players walked out to the "We are the Champions" anthem from the pop group Queen that his side were up against a team who lived up to the song in every sense.

Past greats including George Best and Denis Law congregated inside the ground. There was an unreal feeling to the day, to playing a match with the Championship won and the result irrelevant.

Whatever happened to United the trophy would be theirs at the end of the game. The pressure was off. It was time for carnival football.

Before the game started there was a feeling that United could not lose and even when Kevin Gallacher opened the scoring for Blackburn there seemed no danger.

Giggs soon had the scores level and when at half-time Bryan Robson, the man adored by the fans, came off the bench, the night was complete.

Ince put United ahead before Pallister stepped up and beat Bobby Mimms for a fairytale ending. One man in the crowd summed up the United spirit with the broadest grin in Old Trafford. That man was Sir Matt Busby.

United were lucky they had another game left, another 90 minutes at Wimbledon to enjoy their triumph, and with the vast majority of the 27,000 fans in Selhurst Park that day supporting the visitors it was time for another party.

Wimbledon more than played their part, printing the programme with a picture of Eric Cantona on the cover.

United won 2-1 thanks to goals from Paul Ince and Mark Hughes and when Dean Holdsworth pulled one back eight minutes from time, the United attitude was one of disinterest rather than anything else.

Ryan Giggs and Eric Cantona

The fans refused to stay off the pitch and thereby stopped a lap of honour, but when the players finally made it back through the swarm of people to the dressing rooms, they knew there would be plenty of time to revel in the glory of being the best in England.

The quest for English football's holy grail seemed as fruitless as in any season when United started the 1992–93 campaign with two defeats and a draw. On top of that Alan Shearer, the game's most coveted striker, decided to move from Southampton to Ewood Park instead of linking up with Ferguson at Old Trafford.

And nothing seemed that different in August for United except that the fans were more restless than usual – the title chase had stretched another year and Ferguson hadn't been too active in the transfer market.

A gangling striker called Dion Dublin had arrived, but gone was Mark Robins, who won a place in the heart of the Stretford End as he had the knack of scoring goals at vital times and had been crucial in their FA Cup run and ultimate success in 1990.

Alex Ferguson – always with something to celebrate

History vindicated Ferguson's decision to sell Robins to Norwich, although not in the short term as he started with goals aplenty for his new club. As for Dublin he never got his chance as a broken leg ended his season on his home debut against Crystal Palace.

United's early form didn't really improve and they went into November tenth in the table with Europe, via the Uefa Cup, their initial target rather than finishing top of the pile.

What looked like a sterile season for United suddenly sprang to life when Alex Ferguson pulled off the coup of modern-day football and reignited his team. He brought the most influential player in the British game for decades to Old Trafford. Eric Cantona was at Manchester United!

It was Ferguson's master-stroke. The Frenchman's arrival from Leeds United for £1.2 million was sealed by the chairmen of the two clubs. When Ferguson spoke to Martin Edwards he was stunned by the price they had paid.

Ferguson recalls: "I suggested £1.6 million and then rattled off three or four more figures. Eventually the chairman declared the true fee and I just couldn't believe it.

"Cantona gave us an extra dimension. His impact on United has been immense. He's a wonderful player. It has to rate as the best deal I've ever done."

Cantona arrived in England from Nimes in 1992 and has since led both Leeds United and Manchester United to English league championships, becoming the only player to pick up back-to-back winners' medals with different clubs.

"I belong to United and want to die at this place," said Cantona. "What I like in England is this strong bond that exists between the club and the public, the weight of tradition.

"Stadiums such as Old Trafford have a soul – and I like that. Football in England is alive and people make you really feel it. That gives me a great feeling."

Ironically, the tide had turned for the Reds in 1992 the week before Cantona walked down Matt Busby Way.

Eric Cantona

Against Oldham, with United in mid-table and Norwich and Arsenal setting the pace, they registered their first three-goal haul of the League season.

Two goals from Brian McClair and one from Mark Hughes gave United the win but luckily for everyone at Old Trafford, Ferguson was not convinced or complacent. Along came Cantona to win his second championship in 12 months.

"Eric was the catalyst of the championship victory, it's as simple as that," said Ferguson. "He was born to play at Old Trafford, his genius helped inspire the club to their greatest achievement in a quarter of a century.

"He scores goals, creates goals and dreams up little miracles that are simply beyond the technical scope and imagination of most people. He is the true theatrical performer."

One of the first things Cantona said to the media throng that awaited his arrival was: "We must win at Manchester United." Never before can a player have fulfilled his pledge so accurately.

Cantona's debut, of all matches, was the Manchester derby. He came on as substitute for Ryan Giggs, and inspired United to a 2-1 victory confirming to the fans that someone special had arrived at Old Trafford.

Cantona set United on course for six League wins out of eight matches and one of the two draws in that run was a breathtaking encounter at Sheffield Wednesday when they pulled back from 3-0 down, the Frenchman scoring the equaliser six minutes from the end.

A 5-0 win at home to Coventry on December 28 was quickly followed by a 4-1 victory over Tottenham, with Cantona's fourth goal in as many games, and United were top.

As for Giggs, one of the original Fergie Fledglings, he missed just two matches in 1992-93 and was one of only eight players to start 40 or more Premier League matches. This fact is perhaps the most significant of all in explaining why United finally came good.

So many players playing so many games gave Ferguson the consistency he lacked a year earlier when Leeds pipped his side at the post for the title.

Solid performances are useless in the pursuit of the championship unless you have skill and raw talent to develop skill for the future.

"Ryan Giggs is the greatest talent I've ever managed," said Ferguson as he collected his first title. "He is so gifted Bobby Charlton used to take days off work to watch him, and that was when Giggs was just 14.

"Nobody can manufacture a footballer of Ryan's calibre - his ability is heaven sent."

Ferguson picks out a Giggs special against Tottenham in a 1-1 draw as one of the highlights of that championship season.

"It was a stunner," he recalls. "He pushed the ball through the legs of one Spurs defender, brushed past another with a stunning surge of pace before gliding round the 'keeper to finish from the tightest of angles.

Steve Bruce

"Live until you are 90 and you won't see one better. He's a defender's worst nightmare."

Giggs and his teammates may have been working their magic but the sides behind United in the New Year of 1993 were not taking it lying down. Both Aston Villa and Norwich hauled back precious points before the end of March and United appeared to be falling apart.

United had "bottled it" screamed the tabloids as they had done a year earlier when Leeds won the title. But this time there was a difference – Cantona!

Miserable March soon turned into amazing April and United finished the season better than anyone, 10 points clear at the end after seven successive wins, in which they conceded just four goals.

The rock on which that solid defence was built was Danish international Peter Schmeichel, a European Championship winner.

Ferguson paid just £550,000 for Schmeichel and he says: "Peter has proved to be one of the buys of the century. He saves us 12 points a season."

The most crucial game of that run-in came at Norwich on April 5 when one of their challengers was dealt a massive psychological blow. Cantona, Ryan Giggs and Andrei Kanchelskis all scored within the first 26 minutes and Norwich's brave attempt to win a first-ever championship was over.

Ryan Giggs

That victory stunned the rest of the Premier League and gave United the confidence to go on and claim the crown in style.

The game after that, skipper Bruce stepped into the role of Old Trafford hero with an epic goalscoring feat against Sheffield Wednesday. At that stage Villa were top – by a point – and with the Midlands side drawing at home to Coventry, it looked likely that the gap would grow because Wednesday had gone ahead through a penalty and led up to the 86th minute.

But Bruce scored twice in the remaining minutes to snatch all three points and retrieve the leadership of the Premier League for United.

"I haven't scored for a while and I was due one although I never thought it would come in those circumstances," he said later. "Chris Woods had made some good saves and you got the feeling that we would never score but we clawed our way back in and won.

"I don't know how many times we went behind in that season and come back, but it showed we could fight all the way."

Another important win came shortly afterwards at Selhurst Park. As Villa

Bryan Robson

were losing 3-0 at Blackburn, United pulled off a 2-0 win over Crystal Palace, with goals from Ince and Hughes and an inspirational performance from Cantona.

From then, with United four points clear, it was a question of when and not if the trophy would end up in Manchester.

"Who can forget that night he wrecked Crystal Palace," said Ferguson of Cantona. "His two passes ended in vital goals. At that crucial stage of the championship, nerves were a little frayed. But Cantona was ice cool."

United's inspirational captain for many years, Bryan Robson, was a spectator for much of the championship-winning season, starting just five League games yet Ferguson still had time to pay him a fitting and deserved tribute when the trophy was carefully locked away.

"Bryan had a calming influence on the substitute's bench during the run-in. Keeping him out was the hardest thing I've ever had to do in management, but he was the one who told me not to change the team," said Ferguson.

Ferguson, made manager of Manchester United in November 1986, knew he had at last brought the only prize United really craved back to Old Trafford. No amount of FA Cups or even the European Cup Winners' Cup could satisfy the need for that domestic honour.

"It was only on the afternoon of May 2, 1993, when we were crowned champions, that I truly became manager of Manchester United," he admitted. " That's exactly six years and 177 days after I got the job.

"I wasn't fearful of the sack but winning the League meant there was no longer a threat looming over my work. The burden of history had been lifted from the shoulders of everybody.

"The fact that United had not won the League for 26 years was like an albatross around our necks, but I like to think we have got rid of that now.

"In time people will look back on this side as one of the greatest in United's history. An era when we had some of the best players in the game."

"It's madness to spend half your gate receipts on one player, but what can you do? The others are doing it, so you either join them or get beaten." So said Arsenal chairman Peter Hill-Wood in the summer of 1995, when the club spent a record £7.5 million to bring Dutchman Dennis Bergkamp to Highbury.

And indeed, for a while it did look as though future Championships could only be bought. As Premiership clubs raced to bow at the feet of foreign stars, pessimists in the game bemoaned the cheque-book culture and lack of home-grown talent.

But is the English game really in such dire straits? Of course, world-class stars will always be in demand – nearly every fan wants a Gullit or a Cantona in his team. It's a fact that such players put backsides on seats.

But so does success. And, at a time when transfer fees continue to make the headlines as they spiral ever upwards, a number of clubs have realised the value of a good youth policy.

One of the most exciting developments of the 1995-96 season was the emergence of so many talented young players at Premiership clubs. Foremost of these clubs were Manchester United, who currently have the most promising assembly of youngsters seen at Old Trafford since the glory days of the Busby Babes.

An international encounter, with Phil Neville stretching to check Robbie Fowler

Manager Alex Ferguson is reaping the rewards of a committed policy designed to encourage young players to the club. "I took it as part of my job as manager to watch schoolboy matches and persuade parents they should send their boys to us," he said. "It's a pleasure for a manager to see a bunch of home-grown kids make the grade in his team."

Ferguson is not alone. Liverpool, Newcastle, Tottenham and Chelsea are just some of the clubs now regularly filling first-team places with players who have come through the ranks. Once established in a team, youngsters can provide clubs with the stability and consistency essential for long-term success.

Manchester United, for one, look certain to continue their dominance of domestic football for some time. Ryan Giggs, Nicky Butt and Gary Neville were all regular members of the first team with an average age of 22. With Philip Neville, David Beckham and Paul Scholes also emerging, Ferguson has the nucleus of a side that could still be playing together in the year 2000 and beyond.

It now seems remarkable that, only a year earlier, he was criticised by many for drafting in too many youngsters to replace the likes of Ince, Hughes and Kanchelskis. Critics and fans alike bemoaned the lack of big-name (and high-priced) transfers to the club.

"You can't compete for titles with a bunch of kids" was a popular cry from TV pundits to grass-roots fans. However, as the season progressed, it became apparent that you could do exactly that. United, Liverpool and Newcastle slugged it out at the top of the table even though all three of them fielded players more likely to pack Clearasil than shaving foam for away trips.

Keith Gillespie, Steve Watson, and Lee Clark, all in their early twenties, became regular first-team players at St James' Park and the newspapers had a field day with headlines such as `The Young Ones' and `Child's Play'.

Then, the choruses of "The kids are all right" reached a crescendo when both Liverpool and Manchester United booked Wembley places whilst fielding a number of youngsters in the FA Cup semi-finals. Liverpool's trio of Robbie Fowler, Jamie Redknapp and Steve McManaman displayed a composure that belied an average age of 22 and the United youngsters played like the seasoned pros they are rapidly becoming.

However, it's not just the Premiership that benefits from the recent injection of youth. With so many young players competing regularly in both domestic and European competition, the future of the national team looks rosy. "I cannot recall a more promising group of young English players emerging simultaneously," said Terry Venables. "It is exciting for me and for everyone who wants the national team to succeed."

So will today's young stars be tomorrow's England team? There are certainly enough contenders to fill an England XI for the year 2000. For example:

WALKER

G. NEVILLE   **CAMPBELL**   **DUBERRY**   **P. NEVILLE**

BECKHAM   **REDKNAPP**   **BUTT**   **BARMBY**

SCHOLES   **FOWLER**

(average age in 1996: 21)

In goal, Tottenham's Ian Walker must be one of the favourites to claim a place. Although only 24, he had already made the Spurs No.1 shirt his own. A former member of the Tottenham team that won the FA Youth Cup in 1990, Walker played for England Under-21 before being called up to the senior squad in 1995.

Among his admirers is former England 'keeper Ray Clemence, who thinks Walker is 'a natural.' "He has tremendous ability," says Clemence, "an excellent pair of hands, good reflexes and he's very agile." Walker could well be joined by his Spurs team-mate Sol Campbell.

Although only 21, Campbell had already been called into the England squad after impressive performances for his country at Youth, Schoolboy and Under-21 levels.

A versatile player, Campbell has appeared in any number of positions for Spurs. "A hell of a lot has happened to me in a short space of time," says the former FA School of Excellence graduate, who rose through the ranks of Tottenham under the watchful eye of Terry Venables, then manager of Spurs.

Another graduate of the FA's school in Lilleshall is Nick Barmby, who also rose through the ranks at Spurs.

An outstanding prospect, he had already gained four caps for England by the tender age of 22. He hit the headlines in 1995 when Middlesbrough paid Spurs £5.25 million for him, but he was subsequently out for a while with a knee ligament injury.

On his return, he carried on where he had left off. A superb forward in the Peter Beardsley mould, Barmby went on to be the club's leading scorer in the 1995–96 season, and his best is yet to come. The same could surely be said about Chelsea's Michael Duberry.

Initially a Premiership trainee, Duberry made the first team in November 1995 and since then has impressed all who have seen him play. An excellent centre-half, Duberry was recently described by Alan Hansen as the new Bobby Moore.

Tall, quick and strong, he has flourished under the Continental style of play encouraged by former manager Glenn Hoddle, making a significant contribution to the fluency which Chelsea began to display in the latter part of the

1995–96 season. Not afraid to go forward when required, Duberry hinted early in 1996 that here is a defender who could become a significant play-maker in due course.

Yet another potentially great play-maker is Liverpool's Jamie Redknapp.

Initially a schoolboy at Tottenham, Redknapp joined Liverpool from Bournemouth in 1991 and became the youngest player to appear for the club in Europe when he played in the Uefa Cup game against Auxerre at the age of 18. He has now become an established first-team player for the club and has already a number of England caps.

Redknapp's team-mate Robbie Fowler has also been blooded by England and at the age of 21 had already established himself as one of the most explosive strikers in the Premier League.

He has twice been voted the PFA Young Player of the Year and Venables, in giving him his first England cap in March 1996, predicts great things for him. "He's possibly the best at his age that we've ever had," said the then England manager. "He can shoot with both feet and he delivers his shots very straight and arrow-like. He has very fast feet and the ability to upset defences of the highest quality with his clever runs. The amazing thing is that he will get better as he works on different aspects of his game."

Fowler, Redknapp, Barmby, Duberry, Campbell and Walker – all products of good youth development programmes – are, hopefully, just the start of many young players to come through the ranks. Significantly, however, the remaining five players in this future England XI come from just one club. As Alex Ferguson says, encouraging youngsters has become part of the manager's job. And what rich pickings it can provide!

Paul Scholes, Philip and Gary Neville, Nicky Butt and David Beckham have all come through Manchester United's youth policy. Surely it is only a matter of time before the majority of them become mainstays of the England team.

At only 21, Gary Neville (*right*) was already threatening to make the England right-back position his own.

Calm on the ball, and a good reader of the game, Neville made his international debut in June 1995 and has since become an England regular. He captained United's 1992 FA Youth Cup-winning team and made his senior debut the same year, in a Uefa Cup tie against Torpedo Moscow. A frequent first-team place followed and now he already plays with a maturity well beyond his years.

So, too, does his brother Philip. Although only 19, the younger Neville established his first-team place at United in 1996 and looks likely to join brother Gary as a regular in the England back four.

Both were called into the England squad for the March 1996 friendly against Bulgaria and became the first brothers to play for England since Bobby and Jack Charlton, when they lined up against China in May 1996.

"Both of them have excellent temperaments," says Ferguson, "and I had no hesitation in promoting them both to the senior side despite their youth."

This is a sentiment many share about United's other young guns, such as Nicky Butt, who has already represented his country at youth and Under-21 level. Butt's dogged performances in United's midfield in the 1995-96 season attracted wide admiration and his influence on the pitch is remarkable for such a young player.

An intelligent passer who is not afraid to take a shot at goal, Butt is another of United's FA Youth Cup-winning side from 1992. He made his senior debut in the European Champions Cup tie with Gothenburg in 1994. Only 19 then, he proved to be a fiercely competitive player who won't buckle under pressure. He has since gone from strength to strength and Venables intimated that it would not be too long before he and team-mate David Beckham were called into the senior England squad.

The versatile Beckham came to prominence when he scored the winning goal in United's 2-1 victory over Chelsea in the 1996 FA Cup semifinals. He can play on the right or in central midfield, possesses a phenomenal shot and could develop into one of United's brightest stars.

When only 11, Beckham won a skills competition at Old Trafford and was rewarded with a fortnight's training at Barcelona. Their manager at the time was the ubiquitous Mr Venables! "Even then, I remember being impressed with the boy," recalls Venables. "When I returned to English football with Spurs I made contact but discovered he had gone to United."

However, perhaps the most exciting of all United's young prospects is a player who hasn't even established his first-team place.

Paul Scholes, or "Prince Paul" as some of the tabloids have labelled him, is already being groomed to take over the role currently held by Eric Cantona. At the age of 21, Scholes had already impressed pundits with his "Super-sub" appearances for the club and a scoring average of almost a goal a game.

Ferguson himself has said: "We would never think of selling Scholes – he is just too valuable to our future to contemplate that. He is the player who can fill Cantona's boots. He has great vision and the passing skills to open up any defence. Coupled with that, he has a predator's eye for goal. He can easily slot into the creative role that Cantona has made his own in the last few years."

Cantona Mk II? And English to boot! No wonder Terry Venables spoke optimistically about England's future.

"All these players are making, or have made, the international breakthrough," he says, "and by the time the World Cup comes round in France in 1998, they will have that much more experience and maturity. What I like about the outfield players is their versatility. They can all fulfil more than one role without the quality of their game suffering. It is a really mouth-watering prospect not only for their clubs but for the England team as well."

So maybe the English game isn't at death's door. The aforementioned players are just some of the many youngsters pushing for first-team places at their clubs. As football moves towards the 21st Century, it may soon be that the big transfers in international club football will be away from, rather than to, Premiership clubs.

That should make a few chairmen happy.

It is no good owning the Mona Lisa if you are going to leave it out in the rain and the same applies to footballers. There is no point in spending a million pounds or ten million on the world's greatest footballer to have his strains and aches treated by a saw doctor.

Enter the physiotherapist, the man with literally a fortune in his hands. At all Premiership clubs they tend to be the unsung heroes who, in truth, are as important as any million-pound striker. Arsenal's Gary Lewin is just one of the foot soldiers in this often-forgotten army.

After a decade of liniment in the marble halls of Highbury, Lewin has seen his fair share of bumps and bruises – and he's loved every minute of it even though he is, or was, a would-be professional left to nurse a shattered dream.

As a promising goalkeeper Lewin won county honours with Essex then, in 1980, started a two-year apprenticeship at Highbury. At the end, however, he was released.

Not one to dwell on life's setbacks, he returned to the sixth-form college at his old school determined to improve on his nine O-levels and a year later left with two A-levels and, for good measure, a first-aid certificate.

It was back to Arsenal and a different apprenticeship – this time with that doyen of sporting physios, Fred Street. "Fred took me under his wing at Highbury and he gave me an insight into physiotherapy. I was fascinated," says Lewin.

He was so hooked that he enrolled for a three-year diploma at Guy's Hospital and qualified in 1986. When Street left the Gunners, Lewin was asked to work with the reserve team, gaining valuable hands-on experience. It also allowed Lewin to put some of his ideas into practice.

"I didn't envisage returning to Arsenal so quickly," he says. "I intended to play lower league football and if I didn't make it and get picked up by a top side, then at least I had a qualification to fall back on.

"But then Arsenal offered me a part-time job and I had to pack up playing. I was left to concentrate on my physiotherapy and it has worked out really well."

"When I came here I insisted on having a treatment couch fitted on the team bus so I can treat players on the way to and from away games.

"We also changed the hot food on the coach to pastas. It is also vital you monitor how much fluid and carbohydrates the players take on board."

The advantages of Lewin's regime have been seen on the field where Arsenal become one of the most feared and successful sides in the Premiership. Winning trophies is the job of the players and manager, Lewin's is to educate them in the skills and benefits of his craft.

The pressures, both physical and mental, on Premiership players have increased dramatically and Lewin views a player's diet as an important ingredient on the road to victory.

"The understanding and appreciation of what we do is improving all the time because the clubs are much more professional in their approach," he says. "Players and managers are now aware of the benefits of medicine, rehabilitation, nutrition and diet. That is the biggest plus, on and off the pitch.

"It helps when you have experienced players such as Gordon Strachan and Ray Wilkins, who have looked after themselves, still playing first-team football. Younger players see them as an example.

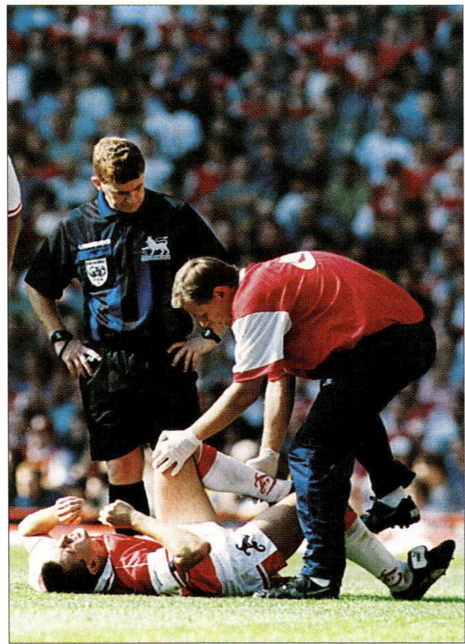

Nigel Winterburn getting the treatment from Arsenal physio Gary Lewin

Fred Street

"From my point, educating young players is crucial. As they come through the ranks you try to drill it home about the value of warm-ups, the warm-downs, the stretching techniques, what they should do before and after the game."

The lessons have been learned by Arsenal who have reaped the rewards and enjoyed European as well as domestic success. When the club travel abroad, Lewin's role takes on an even greater significance.

"Within a day or two of the draw being made for a European tie we send someone out to our opponents' country to carry out a reconnaissance mission.

"We have a full-time travel manager who knows what I want, what the team doctor wants and what the squad wants," says Lewin. "We check everything in the hotel from the beds to make sure they are long enough for the players through to the pillows, blankets and food.

"Do we get sterilised water? Can you get a coach in and out of the hotel? What facilities exist at the airport? A lot of pre-preparation work goes into a foreign trip."

And Lewin is not a man to travel light. "We take everything with us, from our own treatment beds to all our own machinery," he adds. "We will also have made contact beforehand with local orthopaedic surgeons and know where the nearest X-ray facilities can be found.

"We have our own doctors with us and that is important because you need to have someone on hand who is known by the team."

Yet for all the sophisticated equipment, programmes and diets that Lewin has put in place, there are still areas of player fitness that Lewin believes can be improved.

"I would like to see a standard rule in the Premiership that says you can sign a player but he's not allowed to play for 48 hours while medical tests are done," he says. "If clubs sign a player on a Friday morning you've only got about three hours to clear him if the club want him to play the following day and that is not long enough.

"And also the stretcher rule is a disaster waiting to happen because as soon as we get on the field, we are under a lot of pressure to remove the injured player. Why is it so imperative to get a medical person off the pitch when he could be dealing with a very serious situation?

"My biggest worry is that in the rush we will overlook or wrongly assess a bad injury because we haven't had the time to treat the player. It's not right.

"Referees are not medically qualified and players know that to get treatment you have to leave the field. If you're 1-0 up with three minutes to go, and you get a knock, then obviously you're not likely to go off.

"And if it's a serious injury then there is a danger the problem will be compounded by continuing. It hasn't happened yet, but I feel it could. What I would like is more time when I'm summoned onto the pitch."

Lewin's job is not for slackers and he averages around 80 hours per week during the season. Even so, he still loves every minute of those long hours.

"I suppose you end up a bit like a social worker," he says. "You are somewhere between the manager and the players and everyone has got to trust in you. You are caught between the two and handling situations just comes with experience.

"It's been a big help for me being an ex-player, because I know what the players are experiencing and what's going through their minds and what's expected from them.

"As far as I'm concerned I've got the best of both worlds. I'm at one of the best clubs in England, a club that I love, but I haven't got the pressures of playing, of keeping my place in the side. I'm still under some pressure, but of a different kind. That said, I love every minute of it."

HEAD
Always prone to concussion and cuts around the eye caused by clash of heads

CLAVICLE
Fractured clavicle caused by a bad fall on hard ground

HAND
Goalkeeping injury, joint strains, ligament damage, strained thumbs and bruising

ELBOW
A dislocation caused by falling on hard ground

ARM
Broken arms also caused by a bad fall

RIBS
Cracked and bruised ribs from aerial contact

LOWER BACK
Disc problems and muscles strains caused by twisting and turning, running and bending

HIP
Grass burns and muscle strains from the kicking action

HERNIA
A tear in the abdominal wall puts pressure on the groin causing hernia

LEG
Hamstrings, quadriceps, aductors and calf – all prone to strains and pulls

KNEE
Ligament strains or ruptures such as an anterior cruciate tear

ACHILLES
Strains and ruptures caused by pressure

ANKLE
The ankle strain is the most common injury caused by twisting

SHIN
Shin splints and stress fractures due to pressure build-up

FOOT
Blisters, corns and callouses

Ins and Outs – The £1m+ Premiership Transfers

£8.5m – Stan Collymore

£7.5m – Paul Ince

£7.5m – Dennis Bergkamp

PLAYER	FROM	TO	FEE	DATE
Alan Shearer	Blackburn	Newcastle	£15m	Aug 1996
Stan Collymore	Nott'm F	Liverpool	£8.5m	Jun 1995
Paul Ince	Man Utd	Inter Milan	£7.5m	Jun 1995
Dennis Bergkamp	Inter Milan	Arsenal	£7.5m	Jun 1995
Andy Cole	Newcastle	Man Utd	£7m	Jan 1995
Fabrizio Ravanelli	Juventus	Middlesbrough	£7m	Jul 1996
Faustino Asprilla	Parma	Newcastle	£6.7m	Feb 1996
Les Ferdinand	QPR	Newcastle	£6m	Jun 1995
Nick Barmby	Tottenham	Middlesbrough	£5.25m	Aug 1995
Chris Sutton	Norwich	Blackburn	£5m	Jul 1994
Andrei Kanchelskis	Man Utd	Everton	£5m	Jul 1995
Roberto Di Matteo	Lazio	Chelsea	£4.9m	Jul 1996
David Platt	Sampdoria	Arsenal	£4.75m	Jul 1995
Juninho	Sao Paulo	Middlesbrough	£4.75m	Oct 1995
Chris Armstrong	Crystal P	Tottenham	£4.5m	Jun 1995
Jason McAteer	Bolton	Liverpool	£4.5m	Sep 1995
Tomas Brolin	Parma	Leeds	£4.5m	Nov 1995
Lee Sharpe	Man Utd	Leeds	£4.5m	Aug 1996
Ruel Fox	Newcastle	Tottenham	£4.2m	Oct 1995
Emerson	Porto	Middlesbrough	£4m	May 1996
Duncan Ferguson	Rangers	Everton	£4m	Dec 1994
Warren Barton	Wimbledon	Newcastle	£4m	Jun 1995
Sasa Curcic	Bolton	Aston Villa	£4m	Aug 1996
Roy Keane	Nott'm F	Man Utd	£3.75m	Jul 1993

£7m – Andy Cole

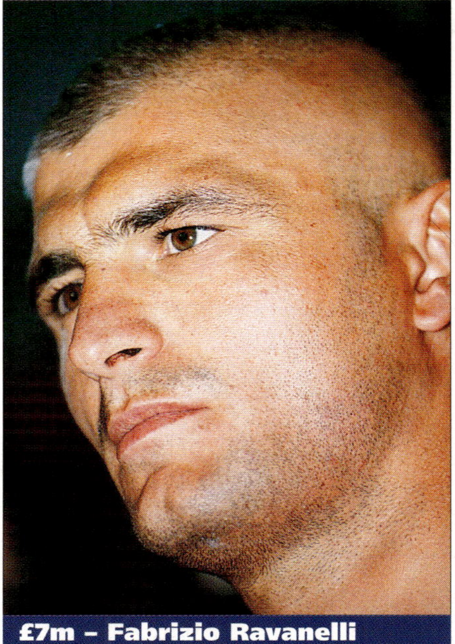

£7m – Fabrizio Ravanelli

£6.7m – Faustino Asprilla

PLAYER	FROM	TO	FEE	DATE
David Batty	Blackburn	Newcastle	£3.75m	Feb 1996
Phil Babb	Coventry	Liverpool	£3.6m	Sep 1994
John Scales	Wimbledon	Liverpool	£3.5m	Sep 1994
Savo Milosevic	P'zan Belgrade	Aston Villa	£3.5m	Jun 1995
Gary Speed	Leeds	Everton	£3.5m	Jun 1996
Karel Poborsky	Slavia Prague	Man Utd	£3.5m	Aug 1996
Patrick Vieira	AC Milan	Arsenal	£3.5m	Aug 1996
Tony Yeboah	Eint Frankfurt	Leeds	£3.4m	Jan 1995
Mark Draper	Leicester	Aston Villa	£3.25m	Jul 1995
Patrick Berger	Borrusia D'md	Liverpool	£3.25m	Aug 1996
Alan Shearer	Southampton	Blackburn	£3.2m	Jul 1992
Gheorghe Popescu	Tottenham	Barcelona	£3.2m	May 1995
Garry Flitcroft	Man City	Blackburn	£3.2m	Mar 1996
Daniel Amokachi	Bruges	Everton	£3m	Aug 1994
Gary McAllister	Leeds	Coventry	£3m	July 1996
Brian Deane	Sheff Utd	Leeds	£2.9m	Jul 1993
Gheorghe Popescu	PSV Eindhoven	Tottenham	£2.9m	Sep 1994
Chris Coleman	Crystal P	Blackburn	£2.8m	Dec 1995
Andy Sinton	QPR	Sheff Wed	£2.75m	Aug 1993
David Batty	Leeds	Blackburn	£2.75m	Oct 1993
Brian Deane	Sheff Utd	Leeds	£2.7m	Jul 1993
Des Walker	Sampdoria	Sheff Wed	£2.7m	Jul 1993
Paul Warhurst	Sheff Wed	Blackburn	£2.7m	Sep 1993
Darren Peacock	QPR	Newcastle	£2.7m	Mar 1994
Stefan Schwarz	Arsenal	Fiorentina	£2.7m	Jul 1995
Andy Booth	Huddersfield	Sheff Wed	£2.7m	Jul 1996
Philippe Albert	Anderlecht	Newcastle	£2.65m	Aug 1994
Carlton Palmer	Sheff Wed	Leeds	£2.6m	Jun 1994
Ilie Dumitrescu	St Bucharest	Tottenham	£2.6m	Jul 1994
Lee Bowyer	Charlton	Leeds	£2.6m	Jul 1996
Terry Phelan	Wimbledon	Man City	£2.5m	Aug 1992
Kevin Gallacher	Coventry	Blackburn	£2.5m	Mar 1993

£6m – Les Ferdinand

£5.25m – Nick Barmby

£5m – Chris Sutton

PLAYER	FROM	TO	FEE	DATE
Neil Ruddock	Tottenham	Liverpool	£2.5m	Jul 1993
Bryan Roy	Foggia	Nott'm F	£2.5m	Jun 1994
John Hartson	Luton	Arsenal	£2.5m	Jan 1995
Gareth Southgate	Crystal P	Aston Villa	£2.5m	Jun 1995
Kevin Campbell	Arsenal	Leeds	£2.5m	Jun 1995
David Ginola	Paris St Germ	Newcastle	£2.5m	Jul 1995
Chris Bart-Williams	Sheff Wed	Nott'm F	£2.5m	Aug 1995
Franck Leboeuf	RC Strasbourg	Chelsea	£2.5m	Jun 1996
Darko Kovacevic	Sheff Wed	Real Sociedad	£2.5m	Jul 1996
Craig Short	Derby	Everton	£2.4m	Jul 1995
Florin Raducioiu	Espanol	West Ham	£2.4m	Jul 1996
Paul Stewart	Tottenham	Liverpool	£2.3m	Jul 1992
Dean Saunders	Liverpool	Aston Villa	£2.3m	Sep 1992
Paul Furlong	Watford	Chelsea	£2.3m	May 1994
Glenn Helder	Vitesse Arnhem	Arsenal	£2.3m	Feb 1995
Dan Petrescu	Sheff Wed	Chelsea	£2.3m	Oct 1995
Nigel Clough	Nott'm F	Liverpool	£2.275m	Jun 1993
Ruel Fox	Norwich	Newcastle	£2.25m	Feb 1994
Paul Kitson	Derby	Newcastle	£2.25m	Sep 1994
Nigel Martyn	Crystal P	Leeds	£2.25m	Jul 1996
Vinny Samways	Tottenham	Everton	£2.2m	Aug 1994
Teddy Sheringham	Nott'm F	Tottenham	£2.1m	Aug 1992
Robert Fleck	Norwich	Chelsea	£2.1m	Aug 1992
Andy Townsend	Chelsea	Aston Villa	£2.1m	Jul 1993
David Rocastle	Arsenal	Leeds	£2m	Jul 1992
Martin Keown	Everton	Arsenal	£2m	Feb 1993
Tim Flowers	Southampton	Blackburn	£2m	Nov 1993
Jurgen Klinsmann	Monaco	Tottenham	£2m	Jul 1994
Klas Ingesson	PSV Eindhoven	Sheff Wed	£2m	Sep 1994
Dion Dublin	Man Utd	Coventry	£2m	Sep 1994
Tommy Johnson	Derby	Aston Villa	£2m	Jan 1995
Glenn Helder	Vit Arnhem	Arsenal	£2m	Feb 1995

PLAYER	FROM	TO	FEE	DATE
Darko Kovacevic	RS Belgrade	Sheff Wed	£2m	Oct 1995
Dejan Stefanovic	RS Belgrade	Sheff Wed	£2m	Oct 1995
Noel Whelan	Leeds	Coventry	£2m	Dec 1995
Eoin Jess	Aberdeen	Coventry	£2m	Feb 1996
Ben Thatcher	Millwall	Wimbledon	£2m	Jul 1996
Georgiou Kinkladze	Dinamo Tbilisi	Man City	£1.9m	Jul 1995
Andrea Silenzi	Torino	Nott'm F	£1.8m	Jul 1995
Jason Dozzell	Ipswich	Tottenham	£1.75m	Aug 1993
Stefan Schwarz	Benfica	Arsenal	£1.75m	Jun 1994
Billy McKinlay	Dundee Utd	Blackburn	£1.75m	Oct 1995
Fernando Nelson	Sp'ting Lisbon	Aston Villa	£1.75m	Aug 1996
Earl Barrett	Aston Villa	Everton	£1.7m	Jan 1995
Dalian Atkinson	Aston Villa	Fenarbahce	£1.7m	Jul 1995
Slaven Bilic	Karlsruhe	West Ham	£1.65m	Jan 1996
Alan Nielsen	Brondby	Tottenham	£1.65m	Jul 1996
Anders Limpar	Arsenal	Everton	£1.6m	Mar 1994
Shaka Hislop	Reading	Newcastle	£1.57m	Aug 1995
Peter Beardsley	Everton	Newcastle	£1.5m	Jun 1993
Julian Dicks	West Ham	Liverpool	£1.5m	Sep 1993
Alan Kernaghan	Middlesbrough	Man City	£1.5m	Sep 1993
Mark Stein	Stoke	Chelsea	£1.5m	Oct 1993
Nicky Summerbee	Swindon	Man City	£1.5m	Jun 1994
Ian Nolan	Tranmere	Sheff Wed	£1.5m	Aug 1994
Don Hutchison	Liverpool	West Ham	£1.5m	Aug 1994
Jeff Kenna	Southampton	Blackburn	£1.5m	Mar 1995
Mark Kennedy	Millwall	Liverpool	£1.5m	Mar 1995
Mark Hughes	Man Utd	Chelsea	£1.5m	Jun 1995
Dean Saunders	Aston Villa	Galatasaray	£1.5m	Jul 1995
Marc Degryse	Anderlecht	Sheff Wed	£1.5m	Jul 1995
Gerry Taggart	Barnsley	Bolton	£1.5m	Aug 1995
John Salako	Crystal P	Coventry	£1.5m	Aug 1995
Mark Hateley	Rangers	QPR	£1.5m	Sep 1995
Graham Fenton	Aston Villa	Blackburn	£1.5m	Oct 1995
Richard Shaw	Crystal P	Coventry	£1.5m	Nov 1995
Ilie Dumitrescu	Tottenham	West Ham	£1.5m	Jan 1996
Andy Sinton	Sheff Wed	Tottenham	£1.5m	Jan 1996
Nigel Clough	Liverpool	Man City	£1.5m	Jan 1996
Julian Joachim	Leicester	Aston Villa	£1.5m	Feb 1996
Liam Daish	Birmingham	Coventry	£1.5m	Feb 1996
Jon Newsome	Norwich	Sheff Wed	£1.5m	Mar 1996
Dean Saunders	Galatasaray	Nott'm F	£1.5m	Jun 1996
Ole Gunnar Solskjar	Molde	Man Utd	£1.5m	Jul 1996
Paul Gerrard	Oldham	Everton	£1.5m	Jul 1996
Paul Furlong	Chelsea	Birmingham	£1.5m	Jul 1996
Mikhail Kavelashvili	Sp Vladikavkaz	Man City	£1.4m	Mar 1996
Richard Hall	Southampton	West Ham	£1.4m	Aug 1996
John Fashanu	Wimbledon	Aston Villa	£1.35m	Aug 1994
Jurgen Klinsmann	Tottenham	Bayern Munich	£1.35m	Jul 1995
Stuart Ripley	Middlesbrough	Blackburn	£1.3m	Jul 1992
Dan Petrescu	Genoa	Sheff Wed	£1.3m	Aug 1994
Mark Rieper	Brondby	West Ham	£1.3m	May 1995
Niall Quinn	Man City	Sunderland	£1.3m	Aug 1996

PLAYER	FROM	TO	FEE	DATE
Gavin Peacock	Newcastle	Chelsea	£1.25m	Jul 1993
Colin Calderwood	Swindon	Tottenham	£1.25m	Jul 1993
David May	Blackburn	Man Utd	£1.25m	May 1994
Tony Daley	Aston Villa	Wolves	£1.25m	May 1994
David Rocastle	Man City	Chelsea	£1.25m	Aug 1994
Chris Kiwomya	Ipswich	Arsenal	£1.25m	Jan 1995
Ned Zelic	Bor Dortmund	QPR	£1.25m	Jul 1995
Eric Cantona	Leeds	Man Utd	£1.2m	Nov 1992
Guy Whittingham	Portsmouth	Aston Villa	£1.2m	Aug 1993
Gordon Durie	Tottenham	Rangers	£1.2m	Nov 1993
Gordon Watson	Sheff Wed	Southampton	£1.2m	Mar 1995
Nathan Blake	Sheff Utd	Bolton	£1.2m	Dec 1995
Neil Shipperley	Chelsea	Southampton	£1.2m	Jan 1995
Don Hutchison	West Ham	Sheff Utd	£1.2m	Jan 1996
Ronny Johnsen	Besiktas	Man Utd	£1.2m	Jul 1996
Paul Telfer	Luton	Coventry	£1.15m	Jun 1995
John Jensen	Brondby	Arsenal	£1.1m	Jul 1992
Peter Beagrie	Everton	Man City	£1.1m	Mar 1994
David Burrows	Everton	Coventry	£1.1m	Mar 1995
Simon Osborn	QPR	Wolves	£1.1m	Dec 1995
Chris Waddle	Marseille	Sheff Wed	£1m	Jun 1992
Dion Dublin	Cambridge	Man Utd	£1m	Aug 1992
Chris Armstrong	Millwall	Crystal P	£1m	Sep 1992
Roy Wegerle	Blackburn	Coventry	£1m	Mar 1993
Eddie McGoldrick	Crystal P	Arsenal	£1m	Jun 1993
Jon Newsome	Leeds	Norwich	£1m	Jun 1994
Joey Beauchamp	Oxford	West Ham	£1m	Jun 1994
John Moncur	Swindon	West Ham	£1m	Jun 1994
Steve Sedgley	Tottenham	Ipswich	£1m	Jun 1994
Steve Froggatt	Aston Villa	Wolves	£1m	Jul 1994
Adrian Paz	Penarol	Ipswich	£1m	Sep 1994
Efan Ekoku	Norwich	Wimbledon	£1m	Oct 1994
Ian Taylor	Sheff Wed	Aston Villa	£1m	Dec 1994
Keith Gillespie	Man Utd	Newcastle	£1m	Jan 1995
Mark Robins	Norwich	Leicester	£1m	Jan 1995
Simon Osborn	Reading	QPR	£1m	Jul 1995
Marco Boogers	Sp Rotterdam	West Ham	£1m	Jul 1995
Mark Atkins	Blackburn	Wolves	£1m	Sep 1995
Sasa Curcic	Part Belgrade	Bolton	£1m	Oct 1995
Richard Jobson	Oldham	Leeds	£1m	Oct 1995
Klas Ingesson	Sheff Wed	Bari	£1m	Nov 1995
Regi Blinker	Feyenoord	Sheff Wed	£1m	Mar 1996
Gary Croft	Grimsby	Blackburn	£1m	Mar 1996
Iwan Roberts	Leicester	Wolves	£1m	Jul 1996
Nikola Jerkan	Real Oviedo	Nott'm F	£1m	Jul 1996
Christian Dailly	Dundee Utd	Derby	£1m	Jul 1996
Régis Genaux	Standard Liege	Coventry	£1m	Aug 1996

£4.75m – David Platt

£4.75m – Juninho

24 FOR THE
PRICE OF 20
ARSENAL WORLD OF SPOR

Can't Buy Me Love – Club Memorabilia

by Sarah Winterburn

The true Arsenal fan wears Gunners underwear underneath his Gunners tracksuit and keeps warm in his Gunners jacket. He has Gunners jewellery, watch and cap and goes to work in a shirt and tie emblazoned with a cannon and will speak only on a telephone bearing the name of his favourite club.

He drinks from Gunners mugs and tankards, writes only with a Gunners pen and his hair has a gloss which can only come from using Arsenal shampoo and coiffing with a Gunners comb. At the end of the day he goes home to his Gunners curtains and wallpaper and sleeps in his Gunners bed. Alone. This is because the single duvet cover does not allow the Gunners man to have a partner.

If he manages to produce a little Gunner, junior will learn to spell while wearing the 'A is for Arsenal' range of clothing and dribbling into the Arsenal bib. Gunner Junior will then go to school clutching a red bag, carrying a red pencil case with red pens, pencils and rubbers and come home to play with the 'Make Your Own Highbury' set.

Any Arsenal fan who does not own all of the hundreds of products on the Arsenal market cannot be a true fan. If he does not wear Gunners deodorant he can fairly be accused of being a closet Spurs supporter. Then he would have the added bonus of a Tottenham camisole and briefs set, available for only £9.99 in black, white or navy. Just don't ask if it comes in red!

Skill and poise are no longer the only key words in football. Add marketing and merchandise as Premiership clubs take millions in the shops to match the millions at the turnstiles. Arsenal's World of Sport shop at Finsbury Park and Manchester United's range of shops across Europe attract thousands of visitors from all over the globe, eager to snap up anything emblazoned with the crest of their heroes.

These include the replica kits, up to three are available for each Premier club and these change with the same regularity as the fashions of Paris and Rome. Blink and you will miss yet another kit being launched and thousands of children protesting that they could not possibly wear last season's kit, or even last month's.

It is not a question of being chic but having street cred and there is none of that for the Tottenham fan still advertising Holsten.

At the start of the 1995/96 season each of the Premiership teams changed at least one of their strips and with prices between £45 and £55 for the full kit – and that is only if you can fit into a child's size – it is a lucrative business.

For the adult version of the team strip you can expect to pay over £60, and that's without splashing out on the crested gold signet ring or keyring, the latter being the better choice for those on a budget, being around £60 cheaper. Success on the field sits side by side with commercial success. Newcastle

Arsenal's World of Sport shop attracts thousands of visitors from all over the globe

United have become one of the biggest teams in English football and as a result business has boomed. You could almost believe that David Ginola was hired as much for his abilities as a model as for his ball skills.

Ginola has helped launch the club's brand of clothing, which clearly should be worn while drinking Newcastle United's own brand of whisky or the ale of their sponsors. You could almost be forgiven for forgetting their skilful brand of football.

But in an age where multi-million pound deals for footballers are commonplace such marketing is required in order to generate enough income to pay for the big names. The sales of Everton toffee probably paid for the signing of Andrei Kanchelskis from Manchester United, a team which gets only forty per cent of its money from gate receipts and the rest through off-field endeavours.

Labour leader Tony Blair targeted them last season as being on the "fine line between marketing and exploitation."

But for those with a West Ham suit cover (£5.99) or a set of Wimbledon car mats (£19.99) there can be no argument against the mass marketing of football. Think of a product, any product, and you can bet your last pound that there is a football club somewhere that has branded it with its logo.

PFA PLAYER OF THE YEAR

1993: Paul McGrath (Aston Villa)
1994: Eric Cantona (Man Utd)
1995: Alan Shearer (Blackburn)
1996: Les Ferdinand (Newcastle)

PFA YOUNG PLAYER OF THE YEAR

1993: Ryan Giggs (Man Utd)
1994: Andy Cole (Newcastle)
1995: Robbie Fowler (Liverpool)
1996: Robbie Fowler (Liverpool)

FOOTBALLER OF THE YEAR
(Awarded by Football Writers' Association)

1993: Chris Waddle (Sheff Wed)
1994: Alan Shearer (Blackburn)

1995: Jurgen Klinsmann (Tottenham)
1996: Eric Cantona (Man Utd)

MANAGER OF THE YEAR

1993: Alex Ferguson (Man Utd)
1994: Alex Ferguson (Man Utd)

1995: Kenny Dalglish (Blackburn)
1996: Alex Ferguson (Man Utd)

MANAGER OF THE MONTH AWARDS

1992-93:
AUGUST: Mike Walker (Norwich)
SEPTEMBER: Bobby Gould (Coventry)
OCTOBER: Ron Atkinson (Aston Villa)
NOVEMBER: Mike Walker (Norwich)
DECEMBER: Steve Coppell (Crystal P)
JANUARY: Trevor Francis (Sheff Wed)
FEBRUARY: Doug Livermore (Tottenham)
MARCH: George Graham (Arsenal)
APRIL: Alex Ferguson (Man Utd)

1993-4:
AUGUST: Alex Ferguson (Man Utd)
SEPTEMBER: Joe Kinnear (Wimbledon)
OCTOBER: Mike Walker (Norwich)
NOVEMBER: Kevin Keegan (Newcastle)
DECEMBER: Trevor Francis (Sheff Wed)
JANUARY: Kenny Dalglish (Blackburn)
FEBRUARY: Joe Royle (Oldham)
MARCH: Joe Kinnear (Wimbledon)
APRIL: Joe Kinnear (Wimbledon)

1994-5:
AUGUST: Kevin Keegan (Newcastle)
SEPTEMBER: Kevin Keegan (Newcastle)
OCTOBER: Frank Clark (Nott'm F)
NOVEMBER: Alan Ball (Man City)
DECEMBER: Roy Evans (Liverpool)
JANUARY: Roy Evans (Liverpool)
FEBRUARY: Alex Ferguson (Man Utd)
MARCH: Alex Ferguson (Man Utd)
APRIL: Howard Wilkinson (Leeds)

1995-6:
AUGUST: Kevin Keegan (Newcastle)
SEPTEMBER: Kevin Keegan (Newcastle)
OCTOBER: Frank Clark (Nott'm F)
NOVEMBER: Alan Ball (Man City)
DECEMBER: Roy Evans (Liverpool)
JANUARY: Roy Evans (Liverpool)
FEBRUARY: Alex Ferguson (Man Utd)
MARCH: Alex Ferguson (Man Utd)
APRIL: Dave Merrington (Southampton)

CLUB PLAYER OF THE YEAR AWARDS

1992-93:

ARSENAL: Ian Wright
ASTON VILLA: Paul McGrath
BLACKBURN: Colin Hendry
CHELSEA: Frank Sinclair
COVENTRY: Peter Atherton
CRYSTAL PALACE: Andy Thorn
EVERTON: Tony Cottee
IPSWICH: Mick Stockwell
LEEDS: Gordon Strachan
LIVERPOOL: Jamie Redknapp
MAN. CITY: Garry Flitcroft
MAN UTD: Paul Ince
MIDDLESBROUGH: John Hendrie
NORWICH: Bryan Gunn
NOTT'M F: Nigel Clough
OLDHAM: Mike Milligan
QPR: Les Ferdinand
SHEFF UTD: Alan Kelly &
    Paul Beesley
SHEFF WED: Chris Waddle
SOUTHAMPTON: Tim Flowers
TOTTENHAM: Paul Allen
WIMBLEDON: John Scales

1993-94:

ARSENAL: Ian Wright
ASTON VILLA: Mark Bosnich
BLACKBURN: David Batty
CHELSEA: Steve Clarke
COVENTRY: Phil Babb
EVERTON: Graham Stuart
IPSWICH: John Wark
LEEDS: Gary McAllister
LIVERPOOL: Ian Rush
MAN. CITY: Tony Coton
MAN UTD: Eric Cantona
NEWCASTLE: Peter Beardsley
NORWICH: Chris Sutton
OLDHAM: Richard Jobson
QPR: David Bardsley
SHEFF UTD: Carl Bradshaw
SHEFF WED: Des Walker
SOUTHAMPTON: Matthew
    Le Tissier
SWINDON: John Moncur
TOTTENHAM: Darren Anderton
WEST HAM: Trevor Morley
WIMBLEDON: Dean Holdsworth

Jurgen Klinsmann

Georgiou Kinkladze

Stuart Pearce

1994-95:

ARSENAL: Tony Adams
ASTON VILLA: Dean Saunders
BLACKBURN: Alan Shearer
CHELSEA: Erland Johnsen
COVENTRY: Brian Borrows
CRYSTAL PALACE: Richard Shaw
EVERTON: David Unsworth
IPSWICH: Craig Forrest
LEEDS: Brian Deane
LEICESTER: Kevin Poole
LIVERPOOL: Steve McManaman
MAN. CITY: Uwe Rosler
MAN UTD: Andrei Kanchelskis
NEWCASTLE: Barry Venison
NORWICH: Jon Newsome
NOTT'M F: Steve Stone
QPR: Andy Impey
SHEFF WED: Peter Atherton
SOUTHAMPTON: Matthew
    Le Tissier
TOTTENHAM: Jurgen Klinsmann
WEST HAM: Steve Potts
WIMBLEDON: Warren Barton

1995-96:

ARSENAL: David Seaman
ASTON VILLA: Dwight Yorke
BLACKBURN: Colin Hendry
BOLTON: Keith Branagan
CHELSEA: To be announced
COVENTRY: Paul Williams
EVERTON: Andrei Kanchelskis
LEEDS: Tony Yeboah
LIVERPOOL: Robbie Fowler
MAN. CITY: Georgi Kinkladze
MAN UTD: Eric Cantona
MIDDLESBROUGH: Steve Vickers
NEWCASTLE: Les Ferdinand
NOTT'M F: Stuart Pearce
QPR: Trevor Sinclair
SHEFF WED: Marc Degryse
SOUTHAMPTON: Dave Beasant
TOTTENHAM: Teddy Sheringham
WEST HAM: Julian Dicks
WIMBLEDON: Oyvind
    Leonhardsen

		GOALS	GAMES	
1	Alan Shearer	112	131	(a goal every 1.16 games)
2	Les Ferdinand	85	146	(1.72)
3	Ian Wright	71	130	(1.83)
4	Teddy Sheringham	69	134	(1.94)
5	Andy Cole	66	109	(1.65)
6	Matthew Le Tissier	66	153	(2.31)
7	Robbie Fowler	65	107	(1.65)
8	Eric Cantona	59	118	(2.00)
9	Dean Holdsworth	53	136	(2.57)
10	Tony Cottee	51	125	(2.45)
11	Peter Beardsley	51	143	(2.80)
12	Mark Bright	49	122	(2.49)

TOP STRIKERS SEASON BY SEASON SINCE THE PREMIER LEAGUE BEGAN:

1992/93

1	Teddy Sheringham	21
2	Les Ferdinand	20
3	Dean Holdsworth	19
4	Mick Quinn	17
5 =	Alan Shearer	16
5 =	David White	16
7 =	Eric Cantona	15
7 =	Lee Chapman	15
7 =	Brian Deane	15
7 =	Mark Hughes	15
7 =	Matt Le Tissier	15
7 =	Ian Wright	15

1993/94

1	Andy Cole	34
2	Alan Shearer	31
3 =	Chris Sutton	25
3 =	Matt Le Tissier	25
5	Ian Wright	23
6	Peter Beardsley	21
7	Mark Bright	19
8	Eric Cantona	18
9 =	Dean Holdsworth	17
9 =	Rodney Wallace	17

1994/95

1	Alan Shearer	34
2	Robbie Fowler	25
3	Les Ferdinand	24
4	Stan Collymore	22
5	Andy Cole	21
6	Jurgen Klinsmann	20
7	Matt Le Tissier	19
8 =	Teddy Sheringham	18
8 =	Ian Wright	18
10 =	Uwe Rosler	15
10 =	Chris Sutton	15
10 =	Dean Saunders	15

1995/96

1	Alan Shearer	31
2	Robbie Fowler	28
3	Les Ferdinand	25
4	Dwight Yorke	17
5 =	Andrei Kanchelskis	16
5 =	Teddy Sheringham	16
7 =	Chris Armstrong	15
7 =	Ian Wright	15
9 =	Eric Cantona	14
9 =	Dion Dublin	14
9 =	Stan Collymore	14

GENERAL STATISTICS SINCE THE PREMIER LEAGUE BEGAN:

BIGGEST WIN: Manchester United 9, Ipswich Town 0 – March 4, 1995

BIGGEST AWAY WIN: Sheffield Wednesday 1, Nottingham Forest 7 – April 1, 1995

MOST GOALS ON ONE DAY: 47 in nine matches on May 8, 1993

MOST INDIVIDUAL GOALS IN ONE MATCH: 5 by Andy Cole for Manchester United v Ipswich Town – March 4, 1995

FASTEST GOAL: 12 seconds by Dwight Yorke for Aston Villa at Coventry – September 30, 1995

FASTEST HAT-TRICK: 4½ minutes (26,29,31) by Robbie Fowler for Liverpool v Arsenal – August 28, 1994

BIGGEST ATTENDANCE: 50,332, Manchester United v Coventry City – April 8, 1996

LOWEST ATTENDANCE: 3,039, Wimbledon v Everton – January 26, 1993

YOUNGEST PLAYER: Neil Finn (West Ham at Manchester City – January 1, 1996), aged 17 years, 3 days

OLDEST PLAYER: John Burridge (half-time substitute for Manchester City v Newcastle, 0-0 – April 29, 1995), aged 43 years, 4 months, 26 days

by Sarah Winterburn

The men in black are back. Premiership referees have given up their green uniforms and returned to their traditional colours for the 1996-97 season. But the changes that have taken place for the men in the middle go far deeper than that.

Terrace abuse used to run along the lines, "Oi, Ref! You're blind." Today the majority of football followers know the referee by name and exactly whose parentage they are questioning.

The Premiership's list of elite officials has made the face of the man in the middle a familiar one; the referee has become a personality in his own right. The likes of Alan Wilkie, Roger Dilkes and Gerald Ashby, to pick three, are no longer just a programme footnote written in small print.

They are courted for their opinions, their steps are watched, recorded and commented upon in newspaper columns. The national newspapers regularly carry `league tables' of the most influential men on the football field, recording the number of red and yellow cards they produce.

Newcastle defender Philippe Albert
and referee Keith Cooper

Joe Kinnear – in trouble for an
unseemly remark about ref Robbie
Hart

The worst offenders are openly condemned and the media calls for their heads almost as a matter of course. As a result of that, the referee now ranks alongside the England manager as one of the easiest targets in football.

There is now a two-tier system. The Premiership list of referees is separated from the Nationwide League by salary. The rewards are high, but so is the pressure.

Each refereeing performance is monitored by an independent observer, whose opinion can result in relegation from the top flight if that referee's rating is less than satisfactory.

The outcome has been a rigid adherence by referees to the rulebook and, consequently, condemnation from managers and players alike. The reason is that football is a subjective rather than objective sport.

Joe Kinnear outraged FA officials by likening Premiership referee Robbie Hart to Hitler, and Kenny Dalglish joined the fray with a call for the days of lower profile officials, condemning one particular decision by Paul Danson as a `disgrace'. It seems there has been nothing but trouble for the men in the middle since they have come under the spotlight and then faced screened action-replays from various camera angles of the moments they would rather forget.

This has been the inevitable progression since the dawning of the Premier League brought saturated television coverage and the ever-present cameras. Philip Don, who retired from refereeing at the end of the 1994-95 season because he could not find the time to give his complete attention to the game, defended referees against the television pundits whose main ammunition is hindsight with the benefit of action replays.

THE GUIDE TO THE
CARLING PREMIERSHIP

"We have grown up with the media over the last few years," said Don, "but what they still can't do is to find a camera position which coincides exactly with the referee's angle."

The fans and the media are more aware of the referees in today's game, and the players come up against the same officials several times in a season, so do incidents carry over to the next time the player and official meet? Bryan Robson appealed to the FA for a different referee after he and other Middlesbrough players had clashed with Paul Danson in a game two months earlier.

"You have to be professional and treat each game differently," says Premiership referee Martin Bodenham. "You cannot hold a vendetta against a player if you have had problems with him before. Generally, the atmosphere on the field is encouraging."

Bodenham believes that the Premiership system is a good one, ensuring that `the cream' of the referees rises to the top. His fellow referees Keith Cooper and Roger Dilkes also feel that the Premiership system works, and problems with players rarely carry over to the next time they meet.

Referees who do rise to the top of their profession are well rewarded. They earn £325 for each match they attend and are given generous travel expenses. Although it is only a part-time job, they can earn more than a lower league professional player.

Bodenham thinks the game and the referee's role has improved in the years since the Premiership was formed. Alvin Martin of West Ham agrees with the first part of his claim: "We are making great strides in every area of football except the referees. With them we are still in the Dark Ages."

It seems that not everyone is convinced that the Premiership elite deserve their place at the highest level. But one thing that everyone agrees upon is that Bodenham and his allies will hold at least as much influence in 1996–97 as big money stars like Alan Shearer and Fabrizio Ravanelli.

Above left: Arsenal's Ian Wright pleads with match referee Keith Cooper
Above: Philip Don

One Season Wonders

Bolton Wanderers' Gudni Bergsson slides to tackle Spurs' Teddy Sheringham

"Glory Days. They'll pass you by in the wink of a young girl's eye." Bruce Springsteen probably wasn't thinking of Bolton when he penned this ode to transient glories, but he might as well have been.

The 1995-96 season saw the Burnden Park club become the fifth team whose taste of the Premier League high-life lasted only one season.

Middlesbrough, Swindon, Crystal Palace and Leicester are the others for whom "Season's Greetings" meant exactly that.

From the glories of promotion to the ignominy of relegation seems a long way to travel in the space of a single season. One minute your fixtures include Manchester United, Liverpool and Arsenal. The next, an away day to Grimsby becomes a highlight.

But "one-season wonders" are becoming a regular fixture in the Premiership, with a number of clubs finding the heady atmosphere of the top flight a little uncomfortable.

In 1992, newly-promoted Middlesbrough came to the Premier League's inaugural season with high hopes: "The stadium is sound, the pitch is excellent and the people are ready for a team they can believe in," said manager Lennie Lawrence. "We can become a club that aims to topple the big boys off their perch."

Unfortunately, it was Middlesbrough who fell off their perch. After a sound start to the season, results faltered. Then, as the team really began to struggle, members of the Boro board started a war of words with each other in the local newspapers.

It all ended in tears. Within months chairman Colin Henderson resigned, Lawrence was sacked and the club were relegated.

The new improved Middlesbrough, inspired by Bryan Robson and including Brazilian star Juninho, have since fared better but a precedent had been set.

While Boro were being relegated, Swindon were marching towards promotion. The 1993 season saw them reach the Premiership after some delightful attacking football.

Inspired by managers Ossie Ardiles, and then Glenn Hoddle, Swindon played confidently and with flair. Insiders predicted great things. The optimism at the club lasted for all of 90 minutes.

A 3–1 defeat at Sheffield United set the tone for the rest of the season. By the end of August, Swindon had lost their first four matches, conceded 14 goals, and were firmly planted at the bottom of the table.

They went on to let in 100 goals – the highest goals-against figure in all four divisions – and were stranded and without hope long before the end of the season.

"Relegation was on the cards for most of the season," said Swindon midfielder Lawrie Sanchez. "So it didn't come as a shock. We just have to bounce back at the first attempt. The fans have enjoyed seeing us play the big clubs - they won't want to see First Division football for long."

The fans got their wish – the following season saw Swindon relegated to the Second Division!

As the Swindon 'keeper got backache from picking the ball out of the net, two clubs were hoping for a return to former glories: Crystal Palace and Leicester had both been in the top flight before. The 1994 season saw them back there. Palace as First Division champions, Leicester after a good run in the play-offs.

Both were looking forward to the new season. Palace's return had led to a boom in season ticket sales as fans flocked back to Selhurst Park, keen to see the glamour games that awaited them, while Leicester fans felt that manager Brian Little was canny enough to ensure them more than just a brief stay in the Premier.

However, not for the first time, events didn't go exactly to plan. A stunned Palace never recovered from a 6–1 home defeat by Liverpool on the first day of the season, while Leicester lost their manager to Aston Villa before the season had really got going.

It was fortunate that no-one in Leicester subscribed to the Hong Kong Eastern Express. In an article on English football, the magazine offered the following opinion:

"It is inevitable that Leicester City will be relegated from the Premier League regardless of anyone's attempt to change that fact."

Rather harsh, considering the article was published before Christmas. But Express readers were not misinformed. Relegation duly followed for both Leicester and Crystal Palace.

With Bolton joining the list of sufferers in May, fans of newly-promoted Sunderland and Derby must be hoping a cure is found. And yet again bidding for a Premiership place via the play-offs were those Premiership masters of the vanishing act – Palace and Leicester.

Leicester took the honours and will for the 1996-97 season enjoy the bright lights of the Premiership. But can they do enough to stop themselves rubberballing back to the First Divison?

Some things never change.

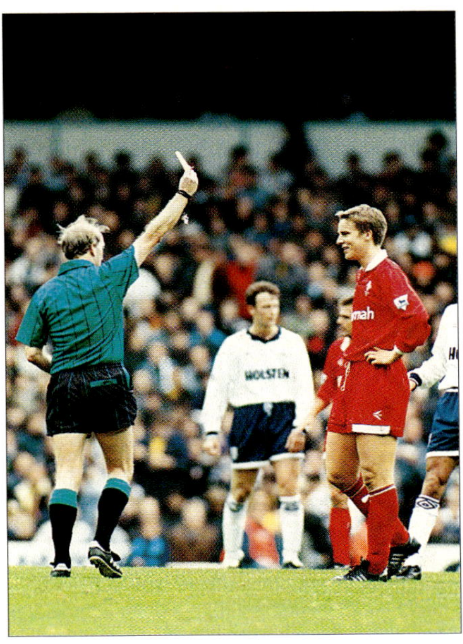

Swindon's Jan-Aage Fjortoft gets the yellow card

Read across for home results, down for away

	ARSENAL	ASTON VILLA	BLACKBURN ROVERS	CHELSEA	COVENTRY CITY	CRYSTAL PALACE	EVERTON	IPSWICH TOWN	LEEDS UNITED	LIVERPOOL	MANCHESTER CITY	MANCHESTER UNITED	MIDDLESBROUGH	NORWICH CITY
ARSENAL	–	0-1	0-1	2-1	3-0	3-0	2-0	0-0	0-0	0-1	1-0	0-1	1-1	2-4
ASTON VILLA	1-0	–	0-0	1-3	0-0	3-0	2-1	2-0	1-1	4-2	3-1	1-0	5-1	2-3
BLACKBURN ROVERS	1-0	3-0	–	2-0	2-5	1-2	2-3	2-1	3-1	4-1	1-0	0-0	1-1	7-1
CHELSEA	1-0	0-1	0-0	–	2-1	3-1	2-1	2-1	1-0	0-0	2-4	1-1	4-0	2-3
COVENTRY CITY	0-2	3-0	0-2	1-2	–	2-2	0-1	2-2	3-3	5-1	2-3	0-1	2-1	1-1
CRYSTAL PALACE	1-2	1-0	3-3	1-1	0-0	–	0-2	3-1	1-0	1-1	0-0	0-2	4-1	1-2
EVERTON	0-0	1-0	2-1	0-1	1-1	0-2	–	3-0	2-0	2-1	1-3	0-2	2-2	0-1
IPSWICH TOWN	1-2	1-1	2-1	1-1	0-0	2-2	1-0	–	4-2	2-2	3-1	2-1	0-1	3-1
LEEDS UNITED	3-0	1-1	5-2	1-1	2-2	0-0	2-0	1-0	–	2-2	1-0	0-0	3-0	0-0
LIVERPOOL	0-2	1-2	2-1	2-1	4-0	5-0	1-0	0-0	2-0	–	1-1	1-2	4-1	4-1
MANCHESTER CITY	0-1	1-1	3-2	0-1	1-0	0-0	2-5	3-1	4-0	1-1	–	1-1	0-1	3-1
MANCHESTER UNITED	0-0	1-1	3-1	3-0	5-0	1-0	0-3	1-1	2-0	2-2	2-1	–	3-0	1-0
MIDDLESBROUGH	1-0	2-3	3-2	0-0	0-2	0-1	1-2	2-2	4-1	1-2	2-0	1-1	–	3-3
NORWICH CITY	1-1	1-0	0-0	2-1	1-1	4-2	1-1	0-2	4-2	1-0	2-1	1-3	1-1	–
NOTTINGHAM FOREST	0-1	0-1	1-3	3-0	1-1	1-1	0-1	0-1	1-1	1-0	0-2	0-2	1-0	0-3
OLDHAM ATHLETIC	0-1	1-1	0-1	3-1	0-1	1-1	1-0	4-2	2-2	3-2	0-1	1-0	4-1	2-3
QUEENS PARK RANGERS	0-0	2-1	0-3	1-1	2-0	1-3	4-2	0-0	2-1	0-1	1-1	1-3	3-3	3-1
SHEFFIELD UNITED	1-1	0-2	1-3	4-2	1-1	0-1	1-0	3-0	2-1	1-0	1-1	2-1	2-0	0-1
SHEFFIELD WEDNESDAY	1-0	1-2	0-0	3-3	1-2	2-1	3-1	1-1	1-1	1-1	0-3	3-3	2-3	1-0
SOUTHAMPTON	2-0	2-0	1-1	1-0	2-2	1-0	0-0	4-3	1-1	2-1	0-1	0-1	2-1	3-0
TOTTENHAM HOTSPUR	1-0	0-0	1-2	1-2	0-2	2-2	2-1	0-2	4-0	2-0	3-1	1-1	2-2	5-1
WIMBLEDON	3-2	2-3	1-1	0-0	1-2	4-0	1-3	0-1	1-0	2-0	0-1	1-2	2-0	3-0

Nottingham Forest	Oldham Athletic	Queens Park Rangers	Sheffield United	Sheffield Wednesday	Southampton	Tottenham Hotspur	Wimbledon
1-1	2-0	0-0	1-1	2-1	4-3	1-3	0-1
2-1	0-1	2-0	3-1	2-0	1-1	0-0	1-0
4-1	2-0	1-0	1-0	1-0	0-0	0-2	0-0
0-0	1-1	1-0	1-2	0-2	1-1	1-1	4-2
0-1	3-0	0-1	1-3	1-0	2-0	1-0	0-2
1-1	2-2	1-1	2-0	1-1	1-2	1-3	2-0
3-0	2-2	3-5	0-2	1-1	2-1	1-2	0-0
2-1	1-2	1-1	0-0	0-1	0-0	1-1	2-1
1-4	2-0	1-1	3-1	3-1	2-1	5-0	2-1
0-0	1-0	1-0	2-1	1-0	1-1	6-2	2-3
2-2	3-3	1-1	2-0	1-2	1-0	0-1	1-1
2-0	3-0	0-0	2-1	2-1	2-1	4-1	0-1
1-2	2-3	0-1	2-0	1-1	2-1	3-0	2-0
3-1	1-0	2-1	2-1	1-0	1-0	0-0	2-1
–	2-0	1-0	0-2	1-2	1-2	2-1	1-1
5-3	–	2-2	1-1	1-1	4-3	2-1	6-2
4-3	3-2	–	3-2	3-1	3-1	4-1	1-2
0-0	2-0	1-2	–	1-1	2-0	6-0	2-2
2-0	2-1	1-0	1-1	–	5-2	2-0	1-1
1-2	1-0	1-2	3-2	1-2	–	0-0	2-2
2-1	4-1	3-2	2-0	0-2	4-2	–	1-1
1-0	5-2	0-2	2-0	1-1	1-2	1-1	–

FA PREMIER LEAGUE – 1992-93

	HOME					AWAY					
	P	W	D	L	F	A	W	D	L	F	A	Pts
Manchester United	42	14	5	2	39	14	10	7	4	28	17	84
Aston Villa	42	13	5	3	36	16	8	6	7	21	24	74
Norwich City	42	13	6	2	31	19	8	3	10	30	46	72
Blackburn Rovers	42	13	4	4	38	18	7	7	7	30	28	71
Queens Park Rangers	42	11	5	5	41	32	6	7	8	22	23	63
Liverpool	42	13	4	4	41	18	3	7	11	21	37	59
Sheffield Wednesday	42	9	8	4	34	26	6	6	9	21	25	59
Tottenham Hotspur	42	11	5	5	40	25	5	6	10	20	41	59
Manchester City	42	7	8	6	30	25	8	4	9	26	26	57
Arsenal	42	8	6	7	25	20	7	5	9	15	18	56
Chelsea	42	9	7	5	29	22	5	7	9	22	32	56
Wimbledon	42	9	4	8	32	23	5	8	8	24	32	54
Everton	42	7	6	8	26	27	8	2	11	27	28	53
Sheffield United	42	10	6	5	33	19	4	4	13	21	34	52
Coventry City	42	7	4	10	29	28	6	9	6	23	29	52
Ipswich Town	42	8	9	4	29	22	4	7	10	21	33	52
Leeds United	42	12	8	1	40	17	0	7	14	17	45	51
Southampton	42	10	6	5	30	21	3	5	13	24	40	50
Oldham Athletic	42	10	6	5	43	30	3	4	14	20	44	49
Crystal Palace	42	6	9	6	27	25	5	7	9	21	36	49
Middlesbrough	42	8	5	8	33	27	3	6	12	21	48	44
Nottingham Forest	42	6	4	11	17	25	4	6	11	24	37	40

	ARSENAL	ASTON VILLA	BLACKBURN ROVERS	CHELSEA	COVENTRY CITY	EVERTON	IPSWICH TOWN	LEEDS UNITED	LIVERPOOL	MANCHESTER CITY	MANCHESTER UNITED	NEWCASTLE UNITED	NORWICH CITY	OLDHAM ATHLETIC
ARSENAL	–	1-2	1-0	1-0	0-3	2-0	4-0	2-1	1-0	0-0	2-2	2-1	0-0	1-1
ASTON VILLA	1-2	–	0-1	1-0	0-0	0-0	0-1	1-0	2-1	0-0	1-2	0-2	0-0	1-2
BLACKBURN ROVERS	1-1	1-0	–	2-0	2-1	2-0	0-0	2-1	2-0	2-0	2-0	1-0	2-3	1-0
CHELSEA	0-2	1-1	1-2	–	1-2	4-2	1-1	1-1	1-0	0-0	1-0	1-0	1-2	0-1
COVENTRY CITY	1-0	0-1	2-1	1-1	–	2-1	1-0	0-2	1-0	4-0	0-1	2-1	2-1	1-1
EVERTON	1-1	0-1	0-3	4-2	0-0	–	0-0	1-1	2-0	1-0	0-1	0-2	1-5	2-1
IPSWICH TOWN	1-5	1-2	1-0	1-0	0-2	0-2	–	0-0	1-2	2-2	1-2	1-1	2-1	0-0
LEEDS UNITED	2-1	2-0	3-3	4-1	1-0	3-0	0-0	–	2-0	3-2	0-2	1-1	0-4	1-0
LIVERPOOL	0-0	2-1	0-1	2-1	1-0	2-1	1-0	2-0	–	2-1	3-3	0-2	0-1	2-1
MANCHESTER CITY	0-0	3-0	0-2	2-2	1-1	1-0	2-1	1-1	1-1	–	2-3	2-1	1-1	1-1
MANCHESTER UNITED	1-0	3-1	1-1	0-1	0-0	1-0	0-0	0-0	1-0	2-0	–	1-1	2-2	3-2
NEWCASTLE UNITED	2-0	5-1	1-1	0-0	4-0	1-0	2-0	1-1	3-0	2-0	1-1	–	3-0	3-2
NORWICH CITY	1-1	1-2	2-2	1-1	1-0	3-0	1-0	2-1	2-2	1-1	0-2	1-2	–	1-1
OLDHAM ATHLETIC	0-0	1-1	1-2	2-1	3-3	0-1	0-3	1-1	0-3	0-0	2-5	1-3	2-1	–
QUEENS PARK RANGERS	1-1	2-2	1-0	1-1	5-1	2-1	3-0	0-4	1-3	1-1	2-3	1-2	2-2	2-0
SHEFFIELD UNITED	1-1	1-2	1-2	1-0	0-0	0-0	1-1	2-2	0-0	0-1	0-3	2-0	1-2	2-1
SHEFFIELD WEDNESDAY	0-1	0-0	1-2	3-1	0-0	5-1	5-0	3-3	3-1	1-1	2-3	0-1	3-3	3-0
SOUTHAMPTON	0-4	4-1	3-1	3-1	1-0	0-2	0-1	0-2	4-2	0-1	1-3	2-1	0-1	1-3
SWINDON TOWN	0-4	1-2	1-3	1-3	3-1	1-1	2-2	0-5	0-5	1-3	2-2	2-2	3-3	0-1
TOTTENHAM HOTSPUR	0-1	1-1	0-2	1-1	1-2	3-2	1-1	1-1	3-3	1-0	0-1	1-2	1-3	5-0
WEST HAM UNITED	0-0	0-0	1-2	1-0	3-2	0-1	2-1	0-1	1-2	3-1	2-2	2-4	3-3	2-0
WIMBLEDON	0-3	2-2	4-1	1-1	1-2	1-1	0-2	1-0	1-1	1-0	1-0	4-2	3-1	3-0

	Queens Park Rangers	Sheffield United	Sheffield Wednesday	Southampton	Swindon Town	Tottenham Hotspur	West Ham United	Wimbledon
	0-0	3-0	1-0	1-0	1-1	1-1	0-2	1-1
	4-1	1-0	2-2	0-2	5-0	1-0	3-1	0-1
	1-1	0-0	1-1	2-0	3-1	1-0	0-2	3-0
	2-0	3-2	1-1	2-0	2-0	4-3	2-0	2-0
	0-1	0-0	1-1	1-1	1-1	1-0	1-1	1-2
	0-3	4-2	0-2	1-0	6-2	0-1	0-1	3-2
	1-3	3-2	1-4	1-0	1-1	2-2	1-1	0-0
	1-1	2-1	2-2	0-0	3-0	2-0	1-0	4-0
	3-2	1-2	2-0	4-2	2-2	1-2	2-0	1-1
	3-0	0-0	1-3	1-1	2-1	0-2	0-0	0-1
	2-1	3-0	5-0	2-0	4-2	2-1	3-0	3-1
	1-2	4-0	4-2	1-2	7-1	0-1	2-0	4-0
	3-4	0-1	1-1	4-5	0-0	1-2	0-0	0-1
	4-1	1-1	0-0	2-1	2-1	0-2	1-2	1-1
	–	2-1	1-2	2-1	1-3	1-1	0-0	1-0
	1-1	–	1-1	0-0	3-1	2-2	3-2	2-1
	3-1	3-1	–	2-0	3-3	1-0	5-0	2-2
	0-1	3-3	3-1	–	5-1	1-0	0-2	1-0
	1-0	0-0	4-4	2-1	–	2-1	1-1	2-4
	1-2	2-2	1-3	3-0	1-1	–	1-4	1-1
	0-4	0-0	2-0	3-3	0-0	1-3	–	0-2
	1-1	2-0	2-1	1-0	3-0	2-1	1-2	–

FA CARLING PREMIERSHIP – 1993-94

		HOME					AWAY					
	P	W	D	L	F	A	W	D	L	F	A	Pts
Manchester United	42	14	6	1	39	13	13	5	3	41	25	92
Blackburn Rovers	42	14	5	2	31	11	11	4	6	32	25	84
Newcastle United	42	14	4	3	51	14	9	4	8	31	27	77
Arsenal	42	10	8	3	25	15	8	9	4	28	13	71
Leeds United	42	13	6	2	37	18	5	10	6	28	21	70
Wimbledon	42	12	5	4	35	21	6	6	9	21	32	65
Sheffield Wednesday	42	10	7	4	48	24	6	9	6	28	30	64
Liverpool	42	12	4	5	33	23	5	5	11	26	32	60
Queens Park Rangers	42	8	7	6	32	29	8	5	8	30	32	60
Aston Villa	42	8	5	8	23	18	7	7	7	23	32	57
Coventry City	42	9	7	5	23	17	5	7	9	20	28	56
Norwich City	42	4	9	8	26	29	8	8	5	39	32	53
West Ham United	42	6	7	8	26	31	7	6	8	21	27	52
Chelsea	42	11	5	5	31	20	2	7	12	18	33	51
Tottenham Hotspur	42	4	8	9	29	33	7	4	10	25	26	45
Manchester City	42	6	10	5	24	22	3	8	10	14	27	45
Everton	42	8	4	9	26	30	4	4	13	16	33	44
Southampton	42	9	2	10	30	31	3	5	13	19	35	43
Ipswich Town	42	5	8	8	21	32	4	8	9	14	26	43
Sheffield United	42	6	10	5	24	23	2	8	11	18	37	42
Oldham Athletic	42	5	8	8	24	33	4	5	12	18	35	40
Swindon Town	42	4	7	10	25	45	1	8	12	22	55	30

FA CARLING PREMIERSHIP RESULTS 1994-95

Read across for home results, down for away

	ARSENAL	ASTON VILLA	BLACKBURN ROVERS	CHELSEA	COVENTRY CITY	CRYSTAL PALACE	EVERTON	IPSWICH TOWN	LEEDS UNITED	LEICESTER CITY	LIVERPOOL	MANCHESTER CITY	MANCHESTER UNITED	NEWCASTLE UNITED
ARSENAL	–	0-0	0-0	3-1	2-1	1-2	1-1	4-1	1-3	1-1	0-1	3-0	0-0	2-3
ASTON VILLA	0-4	–	0-1	3-0	0-0	1-1	0-0	2-0	0-0	4-4	2-0	1-1	1-2	0-2
BLACKBURN ROVERS	3-1	3-1	–	2-1	4-0	2-1	3-0	4-1	1-1	3-0	3-2	2-3	2-4	1-0
CHELSEA	2-1	1-0	1-2	–	2-2	0-0	0-1	2-0	0-3	4-0	0-0	3-0	2-3	1-1
COVENTRY CITY	0-1	0-1	1-1	2-2	–	1-4	0-0	2-0	2-1	4-2	1-1	1-0	2-3	0-0
CRYSTAL PALACE	0-3	0-0	0-1	0-1	0-2	–	1-0	3-0	1-2	2-0	1-6	2-1	1-1	0-1
EVERTON	1-1	2-2	1-2	3-3	0-2	3-1	–	4-1	3-0	1-1	2-0	1-1	1-0	2-0
IPSWICH TOWN	0-2	0-1	1-3	2-2	2-0	0-2	0-1	–	2-0	4-1	1-3	1-2	3-2	0-2
LEEDS UNITED	1-0	1-0	1-1	2-3	3-0	3-1	1-0	4-0	–	2-1	0-2	2-0	2-1	0-0
LEICESTER CITY	2-1	1-1	0-0	1-1	2-2	0-1	2-2	2-0	1-3	–	1-2	0-1	0-4	1-3
LIVERPOOL	3-0	3-2	2-1	3-1	2-3	0-0	0-0	0-1	0-1	2-0	–	2-0	2-0	2-0
MANCHESTER CITY	1-2	2-2	1-3	1-2	0-0	1-1	4-0	2-0	0-0	0-1	2-1	–	0-3	0-0
MANCHESTER UNITED	3-0	1-0	1-0	0-0	2-0	3-0	2-0	9-0	0-0	1-1	2-0	5-0	–	2-0
NEWCASTLE UNITED	1-0	3-1	1-1	4-2	4-0	3-2	2-0	1-1	1-2	3-1	1-1	0-0	1-1	–
NORWICH CITY	0-0	1-1	2-1	3-0	2-2	0-0	0-0	3-0	2-1	2-1	1-2	1-1	0-2	2-1
NOTTINGHAM FOREST	2-2	1-2	0-2	0-1	2-0	1-0	2-1	4-1	3-0	1-0	1-1	1-0	1-1	0-0
QUEENS PARK RANGERS	3-1	2-0	0-1	1-0	2-2	0-1	2-3	1-2	3-2	2-0	2-1	1-2	2-3	3-0
SHEFFIELD WEDNESDAY	3-1	1-2	0-1	1-1	5-1	1-0	0-0	4-1	1-1	1-0	1-2	1-1	1-0	0-0
SOUTHAMPTON	1-0	2-1	1-1	0-1	0-0	3-1	2-0	3-1	1-3	2-2	0-2	2-2	2-2	3-1
TOTTENHAM HOTSPUR	1-0	3-4	3-1	0-0	1-3	0-0	2-1	3-0	1-1	1-0	0-0	2-1	0-1	4-2
WEST HAM UNITED	0-2	1-0	2-0	1-2	0-1	1-0	2-2	1-1	0-0	1-0	3-0	3-0	1-1	1-3
WIMBLEDON	1-3	4-3	0-3	1-1	2-0	2-0	2-1	1-1	0-0	2-1	0-0	2-0	0-1	3-2

THE GUIDE TO THE **CARLING PREMIERSHIP**

NORWICH CITY	NOTTINGHAM FOREST	QUEENS PARK RANGERS	SHEFFIELD WEDNESDAY	SOUTHAMPTON	TOTTENHAM HOTSPUR	WEST HAM UNITED	WIMBLEDON
5-1	1-0	1-3	0-0	1-1	1-1	0-1	0-0
1-1	0-2	2-1	1-1	1-1	1-0	0-2	7-1
0-0	3-0	4-0	3-1	3-2	2-0	4-2	2-1
2-0	0-2	1-0	1-1	0-2	1-1	1-2	1-1
1-0	0-0	0-1	2-0	1-3	0-4	2-0	1-1
0-1	1-2	0-0	2-1	0-0	1-1	1-0	0-0
2-1	1-2	2-2	1-4	0-0	0-0	1-0	0-0
1-2	0-1	0-1	1-2	2-1	1-3	1-1	2-2
2-1	1-0	4-0	0-1	0-0	1-1	2-2	3-1
1-0	2-4	1-1	0-1	4-3	3-1	1-2	3-4
4-0	1-0	1-1	4-1	3-1	1-1	0-0	3-0
2-0	3-3	2-3	3-2	3-3	5-2	3-0	2-0
1-0	1-2	2-0	1-0	2-1	0-0	1-0	3-0
3-0	2-1	2-1	2-1	5-1	3-3	2-0	2-1
—	0-1	4-2	0-0	2-2	0-2	1-0	1-2
1-0	—	3-2	4-1	3-0	2-2	1-1	3-1
2-0	1-1	—	3-2	2-2	2-1	2-1	0-1
0-0	1-7	0-2	—	1-1	3-4	1-1	0-1
1-1	1-1	2-1	0-0	—	4-3	1-1	2-3
1-0	1-4	1-1	3-1	1-2	—	3-1	1-2
2-2	3-1	0-0	0-2	2-0	1-2	—	3-0
1-0	2-2	1-3	0-1	0-2	1-2	1-0	—

FA CARLING PREMIERSHIP – 1994-95

		HOME					AWAY					
	P	W	D	L	F	A	W	D	L	F	A	Pts
Blackburn Rovers	42	17	2	2	54	21	10	6	5	26	18	89
Manchester United	42	16	4	1	42	4	10	6	5	35	24	88
Nottingham Forest	42	12	6	3	36	18	10	5	6	36	25	77
Liverpool	42	13	5	3	38	13	8	6	7	27	24	74
Leeds United	42	13	5	3	35	15	7	8	6	24	23	73
Newcastle United	42	14	6	1	46	20	6	6	9	21	27	72
Tottenham Hotspur	42	10	5	6	32	25	6	9	6	34	33	62
Queens Park Rangers	42	11	3	7	36	26	6	6	9	25	33	60
Wimbledon	42	9	5	7	26	26	6	6	9	22	39	56
Southampton	42	8	9	4	33	27	4	9	8	28	36	54
Chelsea	42	7	7	7	25	22	6	8	7	25	33	54
Arsenal	42	6	9	6	27	21	7	3	11	25	28	51
Sheffield Wednesday	42	7	7	7	26	26	6	5	10	23	31	51
West Ham United	42	9	6	6	28	19	4	5	12	16	29	50
Everton	42	8	9	4	31	23	3	8	10	13	28	50
Coventry City	42	7	7	7	23	25	5	7	9	21	37	50
Manchester City	42	8	7	6	37	28	4	6	11	16	36	49
Aston Villa	42	6	9	6	27	24	5	6	10	24	32	48
Crystal Palace	42	6	6	9	16	23	5	6	10	18	26	45
Norwich City	42	8	8	5	27	21	2	5	14	10	33	43
Leicester City	42	5	6	10	28	37	1	5	15	17	43	29
Ipswich Town	42	5	3	13	24	34	2	3	16	12	59	27

	ARSENAL	ASTON VILLA	BLACKBURN ROVERS	BOLTON WANDERERS	CHELSEA	COVENTRY CITY	EVERTON	LEEDS UNITED	LIVERPOOL	MANCHESTER CITY	MANCHESTER UNITED	MIDDLESBROUGH	NEWCASTLE UNITED	NOTTINGHAM FOREST
ARSENAL	–	2-0	0-0	2-1	1-1	1-1	1-2	2-1	0-0	3-1	1-0	1-1	2-0	1-1
ASTON VILLA	1-1	–	2-0	1-0	0-1	4-1	1-0	3-0	0-2	0-1	3-1	0-0	1-1	1-1
BLACKBURN ROVERS	1-1	1-1	–	3-1	3-0	5-1	0-3	1-0	2-3	2-0	1-2	1-0	2-1	7-0
BOLTON WANDERERS	1-0	0-2	2-1	–	2-1	1-2	1-1	0-2	0-1	1-1	0-6	1-1	1-3	1-1
CHELSEA	1-0	1-2	2-3	3-2	–	2-2	0-0	4-1	2-2	1-1	1-4	5-0	1-0	1-0
COVENTRY CITY	0-0	0-3	5-0	0-2	1-0	–	2-1	0-0	1-0	2-1	0-4	0-0	0-1	1-1
EVERTON	0-2	1-0	1-0	3-0	1-1	2-2	–	2-0	1-1	2-0	2-3	4-0	1-3	3-0
LEEDS UNITED	0-3	2-0	0-0	0-1	1-0	3-1	2-2	–	1-0	0-1	3-1	0-1	0-1	1-3
LIVERPOOL	3-1	3-0	3-0	5-2	2-0	0-0	1-2	5-0	–	6-0	2-0	1-0	4-3	4-2
MANCHESTER CITY	0-1	1-0	1-1	1-0	0-1	1-1	0-2	0-0	2-2	–	2-3	0-1	3-3	1-1
MANCHESTER UNITED	1-0	0-0	1-0	3-0	1-1	1-0	2-0	1-0	2-2	1-0	–	2-0	2-0	5-0
MIDDLESBROUGH	2-3	0-2	2-0	1-4	2-0	2-1	0-2	1-1	2-1	4-1	0-3	–	1-2	1-1
NEWCASTLE UNITED	2-0	1-0	1-0	2-1	2-0	3-0	1-0	2-1	2-1	3-1	0-1	1-0	–	3-1
NOTTINGHAM FOREST	0-1	1-1	1-5	3-2	0-0	0-0	3-2	2-1	1-0	3-0	1-1	1-0	1-1	–
QUEENS PARK RANGERS	1-1	1-0	0-1	2-1	1-2	1-1	3-1	1-2	1-2	1-0	1-1	1-1	2-3	1-1
SHEFFIELD WEDNESDAY	1-0	2-0	2-1	4-2	0-0	4-3	2-5	6-2	1-1	1-1	0-0	0-1	0-2	1-3
SOUTHAMPTON	0-0	0-1	1-0	1-0	2-3	1-0	2-2	1-1	1-3	1-1	3-1	2-1	1-0	3-4
TOTTENHAM HOTSPUR	2-1	0-1	2-3	2-2	1-1	3-1	0-0	2-1	1-3	1-0	4-1	1-1	1-1	0-1
WEST HAM UNITED	0-1	1-4	1-1	1-0	1-3	3-2	2-1	1-2	0-0	4-2	0-1	2-0	2-0	1-0
WIMBLEDON	0-3	3-3	1-1	3-2	1-1	0-2	2-3	2-4	1-0	3-0	2-4	0-0	3-3	1-0

<table>
<tr><td></td><th>QUEENS PARK RANGERS</th><th>SHEFFIELD WEDNESDAY</th><th>SOUTHAMPTON</th><th>TOTTENHAM HOTSPUR</th><th>WEST HAM UNITED</th><th>WIMBLEDON</th></tr>
<tr><td></td><td>3-0</td><td>4-2</td><td>4-2</td><td>0-0</td><td>1-0</td><td>1-3</td></tr>
<tr><td></td><td>4-2</td><td>3-2</td><td>3-0</td><td>2-1</td><td>1-1</td><td>2-0</td></tr>
<tr><td></td><td>1-0</td><td>3-0</td><td>2-1</td><td>2-1</td><td>4-2</td><td>3-2</td></tr>
<tr><td></td><td>0-1</td><td>2-1</td><td>0-1</td><td>2-3</td><td>0-3</td><td>1-0</td></tr>
<tr><td></td><td>1-1</td><td>0-0</td><td>3-0</td><td>0-0</td><td>1-2</td><td>1-2</td></tr>
<tr><td></td><td>1-0</td><td>0-1</td><td>1-1</td><td>2-3</td><td>2-2</td><td>3-3</td></tr>
<tr><td></td><td>2-0</td><td>2-2</td><td>2-0</td><td>1-1</td><td>3-0</td><td>2-4</td></tr>
<tr><td></td><td>1-3</td><td>2-0</td><td>1-0</td><td>1-3</td><td>2-0</td><td>1-1</td></tr>
<tr><td></td><td>1-0</td><td>1-0</td><td>1-1</td><td>0-0</td><td>2-0</td><td>2-2</td></tr>
<tr><td></td><td>2-0</td><td>1-0</td><td>2-1</td><td>1-1</td><td>2-1</td><td>1-0</td></tr>
<tr><td></td><td>2-1</td><td>2-2</td><td>4-1</td><td>1-0</td><td>2-1</td><td>3-1</td></tr>
<tr><td></td><td>1-0</td><td>3-1</td><td>0-0</td><td>0-1</td><td>4-2</td><td>1-2</td></tr>
<tr><td></td><td>2-1</td><td>2-0</td><td>1-0</td><td>1-1</td><td>3-0</td><td>6-1</td></tr>
<tr><td></td><td>3-0</td><td>1-0</td><td>1-0</td><td>2-1</td><td>1-1</td><td>4-1</td></tr>
<tr><td></td><td>–</td><td>0-3</td><td>3-0</td><td>2-3</td><td>3-0</td><td>0-3</td></tr>
<tr><td></td><td>1-3</td><td>–</td><td>2-2</td><td>1-3</td><td>0-1</td><td>2-1</td></tr>
<tr><td></td><td>2-0</td><td>0-1</td><td>–</td><td>0-0</td><td>0-0</td><td>0-0</td></tr>
<tr><td></td><td>1-0</td><td>1-0</td><td>1-0</td><td>–</td><td>0-1</td><td>3-1</td></tr>
<tr><td></td><td>1-0</td><td>1-1</td><td>2-1</td><td>1-1</td><td>–</td><td>1-1</td></tr>
<tr><td></td><td>2-1</td><td>2-2</td><td>1-2</td><td>0-1</td><td>0-1</td><td>–</td></tr>
</table>

FA CARLING PREMIERSHIP – 1995-96

	P	HOME W	D	L	F	A	AWAY W	D	L	F	A	Pts
Manchester United	38	15	4	0	36	9	10	3	6	37	26	82
Newcastle United	38	17	1	1	38	9	7	5	7	28	28	78
Liverpool	38	14	4	1	46	13	6	7	6	24	21	71
Aston Villa	38	11	5	3	32	15	7	4	8	20	20	63
Arsenal	38	10	7	2	30	16	7	5	7	19	16	63
Everton	38	10	5	4	35	19	7	5	7	29	25	61
Blackburn Rovers	38	14	2	3	44	19	4	5	10	17	28	61
Tottenham Hotspur	38	9	5	5	26	19	7	8	4	24	19	61
Nottingham Forest	38	11	6	2	29	17	4	7	8	21	37	58
West Ham United	38	9	5	5	25	21	5	4	10	18	31	51
Chelsea	38	7	7	5	30	22	5	7	7	16	22	50
Middlesbrough	38	8	3	8	27	27	3	7	9	8	23	43
Leeds United	38	8	3	8	21	21	4	4	11	19	36	43
Wimbledon	38	5	6	8	27	33	5	5	9	28	37	41
Sheffield Wednesday	38	7	5	7	30	31	3	5	11	18	30	40
Coventry City	38	6	7	6	21	23	2	7	10	21	37	38
Southampton	38	7	7	5	21	18	2	4	13	13	34	38
Manchester City	38	7	7	5	21	19	2	4	13	12	39	38
Queens Park Rangers	38	6	5	8	25	26	3	1	15	13	31	33
Bolton Wanderers	38	5	4	10	16	31	3	1	15	23	40	29

Copyright of The FA Premier League Limited 1996.
Compiled in association with SEMA GROUP

Saturday, August 17
Arsenal v West Ham United
Blackburn Rovers v Tottenham Hotspur
Coventry City v Nottingham Forest
Derby County v Leeds United
Everton v Newcastle United
Middlesbrough v Liverpool
Sheffield Wednesday v Aston Villa
Sunderland v Leicester City
Wimbledon v Manchester United

Sunday, August 18
Southampton v Chelsea (4.0)

Monday, August 19
Liverpool v Arsenal (8.0)

Tuesday, August 20
Leeds United v Sheffield Wednesday (7.45)

Wednesday, August 21
Aston Villa v Blackburn Rovers (7.45)
Chelsea v Middlesbrough (7.45)
Leicester City v Southampton (7.45)
Manchester United v Everton (8.0)
Newcastle United v Wimbledon (7.45)
Nottingham Forest v Sunderland (7.45)
Tottenham Hotspur v Derby County (7.45)
West Ham United v Coventry City (7.45)

Saturday, August 24
Aston Villa v Derby County
Chelsea v Coventry City
Leicester City v Arsenal
Liverpool v Sunderland
Newcastle United v Sheffield Wednesday
Nottingham Forest v Middlesbrough
Tottenham Hotspur v Everton
West Ham United v Southampton

Sunday, August 25
Manchester United v Blackburn Rovers
 (4.0)

Monday, August 26
Leeds United v Wimbledon (8.0)

Monday, September 2
Sheffield Wednesday v Leicester City (8.0)

Tuesday, September 3
Wimbledon v Tottenham Hotspur (7.45)

Wednesday, September 4
Arsenal v Chelsea (7.45)
Blackburn Rovers v Leeds United (7.45)
Coventry City v Liverpool (7.45)
Derby Couunty v Manchester United (7.45)
Everton v Aston Villa (7.45)
Middlesbrough v West Ham United (7.45)
Southampton v Nottingham Forest
Sunderland v Newcastle United (7.45)

Saturday, September 7
Aston Villa v Arsenal
Leeds United v Manchester United
Liverpool v Southampton
Middlesbrough v Coventry City
Nottingham Forest v Leicester City
Sheffield Wedneday v Chelsea
Tottenham Hotspur v Newcastle United
Wimbledon v Everton

Sunday, September 8
Sunderland v West Ham United (4.0)

Monday, September 9
Blackburn Rovers v Derby County (8.0)

Saturday, September 14
Coventry City v Leeds United
Derby County v Sunderland
Everton v Midlesbrough
Manchester United v Nottingham Forest
Newcastle United v Blackburn Rovers
Southampton v Tottenham Hotspur
West Ham United v Wimbledon

Sunday, September 15
Chelsea v Aston Villa (4.0)
Leicester City v Liverpool (3.0)

Monday, September 16
Arsenal v Sheffield Wednesday (8.0)

Saturday, September 21
Aston Villa v Manchester United
Blackburn Rovers v Everton
Leeds United v Newcastle United
Liverpool v Chelsea
Middlesbrough v Arsenal
Nottingham Forest v West Ham United
Sheffield Wedneday v Derby County
Sunderland v Coventry City

Sunday, September 22
Tottenham Hotspur v Leicester City (4.0)

Monday, September 23
Wimbledon v Southampton (8.0)

Saturday, September 28
Arsenal v Sunderland
Chelsea v Nottingham Forest
Coventry City v Blackburn Rovers
Derby County v Wimbledon
Everton v Sheffield Wednesday
Leicester City v Leeds United
Southampton v Middlesbrough

Sunday, September 29
Manchester United v Tottenham Hotspur
 (4.0)
West Ham v Liverpool (3.0)

Monday, September 30
Newcastle United v Aston Villa (8.0)

Saturday, October 12
Blackburn Rovers v Arsenal
Derby County v Newcastle United
Everton v West Ham United
Leeds United v Nottingham Forest
Leicester City v Chelsea
Manchester United v Liverpool (11.15)
Tottenham Hotspur v Aston Villa
Wimbledon v Sheffield Wednesday

Sunday, October 13
Coventry City v Southampton (4.0)

Monday, October 14
Sunderland v Middlesbrough (8.0)

Saturday, October 19
Arsenal v Coventry City
Aston Villa v Leeds United
Chelsea v Wimbledon
Middlesbrough v Tottenham Hotspur
Nottingham Forest v Derby County
Sheffield Wednesday v Blackburn Rovers
Southampton v Sunderland
West Ham United v Leicester City

Sunday, October 20
Liverpool v Everton (3.0)
Newcastle United v Manchester United
 (4.0)

Saturday, October 26
Arsenal v Leeds United
Chelsea v Tottenham Hotspur
Coventry City v Sheffield Wednesday
Leicester City v Newcastle United
Middlesbrough v Wimbledon
Southampton v Manchester United
Sunderland v Aston Villa
West Ham United v Blackburn Rovers

Sunday, October 27
Liverpool v Derby County (4.0)

Monday, October 28
Nottingham Forest v Everton (8.0)

Saturday, November 2
Aston Villa v Nottingham Forest
Derby County v Leicester City
Leeds United v Sunderland
Manchester United v Chelsea
Sheffield Wednesday v Southampton
Tottenham Hotspur v West Ham United
Wimbledon v Arsenal

Sunday, November 3
Blackburn Rovers v Liverpool (3.0)
Newcastle United v Middlesbrough (4.0)

Monday, November 4
Everton v Coventry City (8.0)

Saturday, November 16
Aston Villa v Leicester City
Blackburn Rovers v Chelsea
Everton v Southampton
Leeds United v Liverpool
Manchester United v Arsenal
Newcastle United v West Ham United
Tottenham Hotspur v Sunderland
Wimbledon v Coventry City

Sunday, November 17
Derby County v Middlesbrough (4.0)

Monday, November 18
Sheffield Wednesday v Nottingham Forest
(8.0)

Saturday, November 23
Chelsea v Newcastle United
Coventry City v Aston Villa
Leicester City v Everton
Liverpool v Wimbledon
Middlesbrough v Manchester United
Nottingham Forest v Blackburn Rovers
Southampton v Leeds United
Sunderland v Sheffield Wednesday
West Ham United v Derby County

Sunday, November 24
Arsenal v Tottenham Hotspur (4.0)

Saturday, November 30
Aston Villa v Middlesbrough
Blackburn Rovers v Southampton
Derby County v Coventry City
Everton v Sunderland
Manchester United v Leicester City
Newcastle United v Arsenal
Sheffield Wednesday v West Ham United
Wimbledon v Nottingham Forest

Sunday, December 1
Leeds United v Chelsea (4.0)

Monday, December 2
Tottenham Hotspur v Liverpool (8.0)

Saturday, December 7
Arsenal v Derby County
Chelsea v Everton
Coventry City v Tottenham Hotspur
Leicester City v Blackburn Rovers
Liverpool v Sheffield Wednesday
Middlesbrough v Leeds United
Southampton v Aston Villa
Sunderland v Wimbledon

Sunday, December 8
West Ham United v Manchester United
(4.0)

Monday, December 9
Nottingham Forest v Newcastle United
(8.0)

Saturday, December 14
Arsenal v Southampton
Coventry City v Newcastle United
Derby County v Everton
Leeds United v Tottenham Hotspur
Liverpool v Nottingham Forest
Middlesbrough v Leicester City
Sheffield Wednesday v Manchester United
West Ham United v Aston Villa
Wimbeldon v Blackburn Rovers

Sunday, December 15
Sunderland v Chelsea (4.0)

Saturday, December 21
Blackburn Rovers v Middlesbrough
Chelsea v West Ham United
Everton v Leeds United
Leicester City v Coventry City
Manchester United v Sunderland
Nottingham Forest v Arsenal
Southampton v Derby County
Tottenham Hotspur v Sheffield Wednesday

Sunday, December 22
Aston Villa v Wimbledon (4.0)

Monday, December 23
Newcastle United v Liverpool (8.0)

Thursday, December 26
Aston Villa v Chelsea (3.0)
Blackburn Rovers v Newcastle United (3.0)
Leeds United v Coventry City (3.0)
Liverpool v Leicester City (3.0)
Middlesbrough v Everton (3.0)
Nottingham Forest v Manchester United
(3.0)
Sheffield Wednesday v Arsenal (5.45)
Sunderland v Derby (3.0)
Tottenham Hotspur v Southampton (12.0)
Wimbledon v West Ham United (12.0)

Saturday, December 28
Arsenal v Aston Villa
Chelsea v Sheffield Wednesday
Coventry City v Middlesbrough
Derby County v Blackburn Rovers
Everton v Wimbledon
Leicester City v Nottingham Forest
Manchester United v Leeds United
Newcastle United v Tottenham Hotspur
Southampton v Liverpool
West Ham United v Sunderland

Wednesday, January 1
Arsenal v Middlesbrough (3.0)
Chelsea v Liverpool (3.0)
Coventry City v Sunderland (3.0)
Derby County v Sheffield Wednesday (3.0)
Everton v Blackburn Rovers (5.45)
Leicester City v Tottenham Hotspur (3.0)
Manchester United v Aston Villa (8.0)
Newcastle United v Leeds United (3.0)
Southampton v Wimbledon (3.0)
West Ham United v Nottingham Forest
(3.0)

Saturday, January 11
Aston Villa v Newcastle United
Blackburn Rovers v Coventry City
Leeds United v Leicester City
Liverpool v West Ham United
Middlesbrough v Southampton
Nottingham Forest v Chelsea
Sheffield Wednesday v Everton
Sunderland v Arsenal
Tottenham Hotspur v Manchester United
Wimbledon v Derby County

Saturday, January 18
Arsenal v Everton
Chelsea v Derby County
Coventry City v Manchester United
Leicester City v Wimbledon
Liverpool v Aston Villa
Middlesbrough v Sheffield Wednesday
Nottingham Forest v Totenham Hotspur
Southampton v Newcastle United
Sunderland v Blackburn Rovers
West Ham United v Leeds United

Saturday, February 1
Aston Villa v Sunderland
Blackburn Rovers v West Ham United
Derby County v Liverpool
Everton v Nottingham Forest
Leeds United v Arsenal
Manchester United v Southampton
Newcastle United v Leicester City
Sheffield Wednesday v Coventry City
Tottenham Hotspur v Chelsea
Wimbledon v Middlesbrough

Saturday, February 15
Aston Villa v Coventry City
Blackburn Rovers v Nottingham Forest
Derby County v West Ham United
Everton v Leicester City
Leeds United v Southampton
Manchester United v Middlesbrough
Newcastle United v Chelsea
Sheffield Wednesday v Sunderland
Tottenham Hotspur v Arsenal
Wimbledon v Liverpool

Saturday, February 22
Arsenal v Wimbledon
Chelsea v Manchester United
Coventry City v Everton
Leicester City v Derby County
Liverpool v Blackburn Rovers
Middlesbrough v Newcastle United
Nottingham Forest v Aston Villa
Southampton v Sheffield Wednesday
Sunderland v Leeds United
West Ham United v Tottenham Hotspur

Saturday, March 1
Aston Villa v Liverpool
Blackburn Rovers v Sunderland
Derby County v Chelsea
Everton v Arsenal
Leeds United v West Ham United
Manchester United v Coventry City
Newcastle United v Southampton
Sheffield Wednesday v Middlesbrough
Tottenham Hotspur v Nottingham Forest
Wimbledon v Leicester City

Tuesday, March 4
Arsenal v Manchester United (7.45)
Sunderland v Tottenham Hotspur (7.45)

Wednesday, March 5
Chelsea v Blackburn Rovers (7.45)
Coventry City v Wimbledon (7.45)
Leicester City v Aston Villa (7.45)
Liverpool v Leeds United (7.45)
Middlesbrough v Derby County (7.45)
Nottingham Forest v Sheffield Wednesday
(7.45)
Southampton v Everton
West Ham United v Newcastle United
(7.45)

Saturday, March 8
Arsenal v Nottingham Forest
Coventry City v Leicester City
Derby County v Southampton
Leeds United v Everton
Liverpool v Newcastle United
Middlesbrough v Blackburn Rovers
Sheffield Wednesday v Tottenham Hotspur
Sunderland v Manchester United
West Ham United v Chelsea
Wimbledon v Aston Villa

Saturday, March 15
Aston Villa v West Ham United
Blackburn Rovers v Wimbledon
Chelsea v Sunderland
Everton v Derby County
Leicester City v Middlesbrough
Manchester United v Sheffield Wednesday
Newcastle United v Coventry City
Nottingham Forest v Liverpool
Southampton v Arsenal
Tottenham Hotspur v Leeds United

Saturday, March 22
Arsenal v Liverpool

Blackburn Rovers v Aston Villa
Coventry City v West Ham United
Derby County v Tottenham Hotspur
Everton v Manchester United
Middlesbrough v Chelsea
Sheffield Wednesday v Leeds United
Southampton v Leicester City
Sunderland v Nottingham Forest
Wimbledon v Newcastle United

Saturday, March 29
Aston Villa v Sheffield Wednesday
Chelsea v Southampton
Leeds United v Derby County
Leicester City v Sunderland
Liverpool v Middlesbrough
Manchester United v Wimbledon
Newcastle United v Everton
Nottingham Forest v Coventry City
Tottenham Hotspur v Blackburn Rovers
West Ham United v Arsenal

Saturday, April 5
Aston Villa v Everton
Chelsea v Arsenal
Leeds United v Blackburn Rovers
Leicester City v Sheffield Wednesday
Liverpool v Coventry City
Manchester United v Derby County
Newcastle United v Sunderland
Nottingham Forest v Southampton
Tottenham Hotspur v Wimbledon
West Ham United v Middlesbrough

Saturday, April 12
Arsenal v Leicester City
Blackburn Rovers v Manchester United
Coventry City v Chelsea
Derby County v Aston Villa
Everton v Tottenham Hotspur
Middlesbrough v Nottingham Forest
Sheffield Wednesday v Newcastle United
Southampton v West Ham United
Sunderland v Liverpool
Wimbledon v Leeds United

Saturday, April 19
Arsenal v Blackburn Rovers
Aston Villa v Tottenham Hotspur
Chelsea v Leicester City
Liverpool v Manchester United
Middlesbrough v Sunderland
Newcastle United v Derby County
Nottingham Forest v Leeds United
Sheffield Wednesday v Wimbledon
Southampton v Coventry City
West Ham United v Everton

Tuesday, April 22
Blackburn Rovers v Sheffield Wednesday
   (7.45)
Leeds United v Aston Villa (7.45)
Sunderland v Southampton (7.45)
Wimbledon v Chelsea (7.45)

Wednesday, April 23
Coventry City v Arsenal (7.45)

Derby County v Nottingham Forest (7.45)
Everton v Liverpool (7.45)
Leicester City v West Ham United (7.45)
Manchester United v Newcastle United
   (8.0)
Tottenham Hotspur v Middlesbrough
   (7.45)

Saturday, May 3
Arsenal v Newcastle United
Chelsea v Leeds United
Coventry City v Derby County
Leicester City v Manchester United
Liverpool v Tottenham Hotspur
Middlesbrough v Aston Villa
Nottingham Forest v Wimbledon
Southampton v Blackburn Rovers
Sunderland v Everton
West Ham United v Sheffield Wednesday

Sunday, May 11
Aston Villa v Southampton (4.0)
Blackburn Rovers v Leicester City (4.0)
Derby County v Arsenal (4.0)
Everton v Chelsea (4.0)
Leeds United v Middlesbrough (4.0)
Manchester United v West Ham United
   (4.0)
Newcastle United v Nottingham Forest
   (4.0)
Sheffield Wednesday v Liverpool (4.0)
Tottenham Hotspur v Coventry City (4.0)
Wimbledon v Sunderland (4.0)

1996-97 FA CARLING PREMIERSHIP PRIZE MONEY

1995-96 in brackets

1. £2,114,300 (£983,300)	8. £1,374,295 (£639,145)	17. £442,860 (£196,660)
2. £2,008,585 (£934,135)	9. £1,268,580 (£589,980)	18. £317,145 (£147,495)
3. £1,902,870 (£884,970)	10. £1,162,865 (£540,815)	19. £211,430 (£98,330)
4. £1,797,155 (£835,805)	11. £1,057,150 (£491,650)	20. £105,715 (£49,165)
5. £1,691,440 (£786,640)	12. £951,435 (£442,485)	
6. £1,585,725 (£737,475)	13. £845,720 (£393,320)	
7. £1,480,010 (£688,310)	14. £740,005 (£344,155)	**TOTAL FOR 1996-97: £22,220,150**
	15. £634,290 (£294,990)	
	16. £528,575 (£245,825)	TOTAL FOR 1995-96: £10,324,650